T0367303

# FOUND TREASURE

# FOUND TREASURE

Gems of Great Leadership and Personal Skills

## Lloyd "Skip" Amstrup

OPEN BOOK EDITIONS
A Berrett-Koehler Partner

iUniverse®

FOUND TREASURE
GEMS OF GREAT LEADERSHIP AND PERSONAL SKILLS

Copyright © 2017 Lloyd "Skip" Amstrup.

All rights reserved. No part of this book may be used or reproduced by any means, graphic, electronic, or mechanical, including photocopying, recording, taping or by any information storage retrieval system without the written permission of the author except in the case of brief quotations embodied in critical articles and reviews.

iUniverse books may be ordered through booksellers or by contacting:

iUniverse
1663 Liberty Drive
Bloomington, IN 47403
www.iuniverse.com
1-800-Authors (1-800-288-4677)

Because of the dynamic nature of the Internet, any web addresses or links contained in this book may have changed since publication and may no longer be valid. The views expressed in this work are solely those of the author and do not necessarily reflect the views of the publisher, and the publisher hereby disclaims any responsibility for them.

Any people depicted in stock imagery provided by Thinkstock are models, and such images are being used for illustrative purposes only.
Certain stock imagery © Thinkstock.

ISBN: 978-1-5320-1093-4 (sc)
ISBN: 978-1-5320-1094-1 (hc)
ISBN: 978-1-5320-1092-7 (e)

Library of Congress Control Number: 2016921381

Print information available on the last page.

iUniverse rev. date: 01/25/2017

This book is dedicated to my greatest role model,
Irving S. Amstrup, my father.
His love is endless.

# CONTENTS

# INTRODUCTION

Welcome to a very exciting book that will allow you to identify your personal and leadership skills, which will help you to assess your current strengths as well as offer valuable insights into how you can easily expand or develop new techniques to enrich your professional and personal lives.

All the things you desire can be yours through a heightened level of awareness, supported by learned methods that will enhance your personal relationships, bringing you greater success and personal satisfaction.

I suspect that curiosity was your prime motivator when you picked up this book or looked at it online. *Who doesn't like a treasure hunt, especially one that offers the secrets to your personal and professional success?* You may be feeling a need to get a better grip on your awareness, improve your personal and professional lives, and make wise choices for your future. Many of the formulas used in this book start with the magical letter *f*. Not foul or nasty words. Indeed, many of the fabulous and powerful *f* words define who you are and what you aspire to accomplish in your life.

These words create a core of important concepts that you can use in business situations, your personal life, or leadership roles.

Here is a list of words we will explore:

- *failure*—the greatest teacher of all
- *faith*—the ability to still believe, despite challenges and hardships
- *family*—the primary motivation for all of our actions
- *fear*—the roadblock to success and happiness
- *feelings*—the emotions that make us human
- *flexibility*—the skill of adapting and evolving

- *focus*—the narrowness of passionate determination
- *forgiveness*—the release of hurts of the past
- *framework*—the processes we design that define our standards
- *freedom*—the God-given right of choice
- *friend*—the community of man
- *fruitfulness*—the purpose of each day
- *fundamentals*—the elements needed by everyone
- *funniness*—the art of identifying the lightness of life
- *future*—the consequences of yesterday and the many surprises of tomorrow

I have spent my entire life in the grateful service of others as a teacher, coach, salesperson, boss, parent, and leader. During my life, I have also devoted a great deal of my time and energy to observing others. This is what I affectionately call *awareness*. I have spent time being aware of the needs and actions of others: what worked, what turned people off, what created enthusiasm, what killed motivation, when people felt good, and when people dipped to all-time lows.

I have lived my life on the premise that everyone is worthy of my time, which is the only gift I really have to share my attention focused on the need of the person seeking my help.

Through the years, I have determined that I have three daily personal goals:

1. Learn something every day
2. Teach something every day
3. Perform a random act of kindness with no expectation of reward or recognition every day

You may find these three goals suitable for your own use. If not, design your daily objectives that will help you make each day valuable and rewarding.

## How the Book Is Organized

You may be the kind of reader who wants to start at the beginning and plough through to the end. That, of course, is probably the best way to get the full value of this book's contents.

If you have an immediate priority that needs attention, it might be advisable for you to review the table of contents and then move directly to the information you desire.

This is your journey, so use the material to your best advantage.

Each chapter will feature an *f*-word that contributes to your personal success. These words will form the basis for your new realities. Use these words as your observation guide when viewing the behavior of others. Remember: *life is a classroom for the aware.*

## Timeless Wisdom

Some background is needed to set the proper tone and the purpose of the timeless wisdom quotes.

My adventurous grandfather came to the United States from Denmark by signing onto a commercial ship as a merchant marine. My grandmother also immigrated to the United States to escape the famine in Denmark in the early 1900's. She came as a sponsored immigrant and served as a governess for a wealthy American family. She was the only one in her family of thirteen siblings to come to the United States.

It took great courage for them to leave everything and everyone behind in Denmark and come to the land of opportunity and liberty, the United States of America.

My grandparents met in San Francisco, fell in love, and married.

My grandfather did not have a great deal of education, but he was a hard worker and determined to become an American citizen. He wanted to live the American dream. With limited transferable skills to offer an employer, he was compelled to take menial and difficult jobs while he built his experience and reputation. He never asked for help; he wanted to earn his own way.

Although he never became famous, he was able to enjoy a very good life. His goal was to give his only child, my dad, a life better than his own.

My father was not raised in a wealthy home, but his father adequately provided for the family. In the spirit of his father's wishes, my father was able to go the University of California Berkeley, where he received a four-year degree in public administration, at a point in time when possessing a college degree was a rarity.

My father, unquestionably the greatest man I have ever known, graduated from the University of California Berkeley just before the unexpected Japanese attack on Pearl Harbor. He volunteered for the navy, where he was earmarked as officer material because of his college education. He spent four years in the Pacific, away from his new bride, fighting to push back the Japanese. He ended the war with the rank of lieutenant commander. Not bad for a young man who could not swim.

He returned to San Francisco and to his bride, who had waited for his return for four lonely years. He got a job and began building his family. Before too long, he had two boys and two girls. With six people to support, he worked very hard and put in very long hours. My mom worked at home, raising four kids and managing the household affairs.

Dad never made an income more than $50,000 a year, but he was a valued sales representative and manager for his company for his entire career. He was known for his loyalty, his ability to think fast on his feet, his leadership, and his wonderful people skills.

Later in life, he became mayor of the city of Burlingame, a small community south of San Francisco. He loved his city. He served on the city council and as mayor for more than twenty years.

His dream for his children was that they would have a better life than he'd had. All four of his kids earned four-year college degrees. Three became teachers, with the fourth going into probation and law enforcement. Each married and had children.

Dad is gone now, having passed away at the age of ninety-three, following Mom, who passed about seven years earlier. He accomplished his dream and passed on knowing the world was a better place because of his presence.

I grew up wanting the same American dream for my children and now for my grandchildren. I started work at age thirteen, working in a warehouse while going to school. I had to pay for my own college education by working numerous jobs while carrying a full academic load. My father taught me to be a responsible, hardworking, and an ethical person, which has served me well. He taught me how to love and lead. I repaid him for his kindness and love by being a good man. I am very flawed, like everyone else, but I kept his dream alive by giving my children a wonderful life. They are currently living out that same dream with their families.

I can say proudly that I have never been unemployed. I learned how to be invaluable to my employers, never giving them reason to discontinue my employment.

Unemployment today should bring neither blame or shame. With outsourcing, tough economies, and emphasis on automation and profits, unemployment is a true reality for many. The American dream has become very tarnished by modern-day challenges, but the legacy of the current generation making the next generation better by working hard and making sacrifices still remains.

So now that I have given you a brief peek into my life, you must be asking why. Simply put, the true values that made America great were identified and articulated by men like my grandfather and father. From nothing, they built a legacy that extends through four generations, with the same goal of opportunity and advancement.

No doubt some of this book's more mature readers will have similar stories. They can also recall the wisdom that was given to children from both mothers and fathers. That wisdom is every bit as valuable today as it was all those years ago.

At the end of each chapter you will find three pearls of wisdom and an accompanying interpretation. Use this traditional wisdom to forge your future.

# The Journey Begins

Do you want to be successful in all of your endeavors? Are you willing to accept the reality of your present situation? Do you have the desire and determination to make needed changes to alter your future? Are you willing to develop the characteristics that are needed to achieve a successful role as a business and personal leader?

The lack of these particular traits can limit an individual's potential for professional success, as well as his or her ability to build meaningful sustainable relationships.

The great news is that these skills can be learned by anyone who has a sincere desire to turn his or her internal potential into reality.

This is the beginning of your journey to view things differently and adjust your thinking in order to bring you better results in business and greater joy in your personal life, and to help you become a positive force in molding the future of the human experience.

Your lessons of the past serve as the road map to your future. You can only complete a meaningful life journey if you have an accurate picture of your destination. The journey simply determines that destination.

The most important skill that is repeatedly discussed throughout this book is the need for each reader to become more *observant*.

Being aware of what works and what causes people to fail will help you

1

define who you truly want to be. It will motivate you to make meaningful, needed changes that will enrich your life. It will encourage you to abandon habits that have hindered your path or that are simply not working.

Let me share a few examples of how *awareness* can be life altering.

### Story: Tom's Weight Problem

Tom is a forty-five-year-old married man with three children. He works long hours to support his family. He is an engineer, so his job is not physically demanding, but it is mentally stressful. He has little time to devote to his personal health or exercising. He eats on the run, often consumes fast food, and is addicted to sugary sodas—his drink of choice. At the end of the day, he settles into his comfortable chair to let his busy mind be numbed by television.

The result of this very common lifestyle is thirty-five unwanted pounds. Each attempt at dieting seems to lead to minor improvement that soon leads to even more weight gain.

On the other hand, his coworker John remains trim even though his life scenario parallels that of Tom's.

Tom begins to watch John's routine.

John never drinks soda. He consumes water often, with an occasional cup of hot tea. He gets up about once an hour to stretch or simply walk around a little. He never eats at his desk. He religiously takes a fifteen-minute break in both midmorning and midafternoon. During his breaks he snacks on veggies brought from home, which he eats in the break room. About three times a week, John takes a brisk walk outside during his lunch break. His lunch is relatively low in carbohydrates, replaced by small portions of protein and fruit.

When asked, Tom reveals that he has a glass of red wine during dinner. He limits his daily carbohydrate intake, replacing them with steamed vegetables, fruit, salad greens, and a moderate amount of meat. He spends his after-dinner hours walking the family dog and working on his woodworking hobby in the garage.

Tom wisely realizes that to become thin, he can simply mimic the habits of a thin person. None of these changes require tremendous sacrifice. Tom needed to overhaul his daily behaviors.

## *Story: An Exercise in Leadership*

A meeting of the customer service and sales representatives of Harris, Burns, and Milestone Real Estate was held last evening to discuss the sales results of the last quarter.

The evening began with friendly bantering among the attendees. The most experienced representative is Sam Dowd, a fifteen-year employee. Sam's experience is always valued, especially by the younger reps. Tom Wiley, a born salesman, has been with the firm for five years. His smooth manner and efficiency make him the top salesperson on the team. Maryann Tabbs, Gaylord Singh, and Ruth Morris have all been with the company for two to three years.

Matt Long looked on in silent observation, having been on the team a mere ninety days.

At 6:05 p.m., the door flew open, revealing the blustery owner, Mike Harris, closely followed by his partner Ken Milestone. The room became very silent as the meeting began.

"I normally like to give some recognition at the start of our meetings, but with our lousy sales last month, there is literally nothing to praise!" Mike said.

"We aren't running a charity here," Ken said and then quickly added, "If sales don't improve immediately, there will be fewer faces in this room at our next meeting."

The meeting proceeded for about thirty minutes with very little input from the sales force.

Only Tom Wiley spoke up: "We have had a hard time closing sales because the local factory is rumored to be in trouble. Many think that they will file bankruptcy and terminate most, if not all, the workers. People are afraid, so they're shying away from making a commitment."

Mike's nostrils flared and his face reddened. He responded gruffly, "We have heard these rumors for years. Nothing has ever happened. Stop the excuse making and work harder."

The meeting came to an abrupt end with both partners leaving the room. Unlike previous meetings, the reps made no mention of meeting at the local tavern for a beer. Everyone appeared rattled or angry. No one looked forward to coming to work the following day.

As the novice in the group, Matt's head was spinning with questions.

What he had actually thought to be an ideal job that promised a great future was now giving him serious doubts.

Mike and Ken, as the leaders of this group, had been derailed by the poor sales results. They were dictatorial in their approach. They did not seek input or calmly seek to understand the performance dynamics encountered by the team. They dominated the meeting with demands, threats, and aggression.

The meeting, which was to have been a review of sales results, had become a demeaning lecture. None of the employees saw the meeting as helpful or motivational.

These two examples contain great lessons for an aware observer. They demonstrate what works and what fails.

Tom found his weight loss answers without any gym enrollment, expensive food management plan, or the purchase of unnecessary weight loss supplements. He visualized himself as a thin person. He identified John as a typical example of what he wanted to be. He observed John's behaviors and mimicked his methods to start his weight loss plan.

Matt learned a great deal by observing the negativity of his sales meeting. He saw his congenial sales leaders emotionally hijacked by pressures caused by poor sales. He experienced a heightened level of stress from the threats that were made. He walked away doubting the value of his relationship with the firm. Most frustrating of all, Matt did not get any guidance on how he or the others could actually improve their sales performance. The meeting was depressing instead of uplifting.

No doubt each of you has encountered similar situations in both your personal and work lives. These experiences can be invaluable if you use them as building blocks to a better you.

Through the following chapters, you will be given coping skills and leadership insights to help you mold a new version of who you truly want to be. This will enable you to recreate yourself. It will also help you realize your strengths as well as areas in need of improvement.

Your journey will help your *awareness* skills via simple *observation* and *analysis*. With your newfound abilities, you will enhance every aspect of your life.

During your reading experience, you will come across many interesting stories to illustrate the significant points that are expressed. Storytelling is an art form that is being lost today in our new world of texting, e-mails, and lack of oral communication. It is hurting all of us. Our brains visualize in the form of pictures and stories. Stories give a storyteller the opportunity to change emotions, bring humor to the experience, and impart knowledge. Who does not remember a funny joke or two? That's the point: You remember things that make you smile. You remember things that make you cry. You remember the moments in your life when your heart is touched by emotion, be it the birth of a baby, the loss of a loved one, or the joy of accomplishment when you see a person rise above his or her limitations to achieve what appears to be an unreachable goal.

You see, life is good! It is filled with moments that allow you to use and develop your full range of emotions.

It's time to shed your negative thoughts! It is time to truly realize you were created with all of the important characteristics necessary to live a full, rich, successful, and meaningful life.

So let your journey begin! Realize that you are the master of your personal destiny. Never surrender that journey or experience to anyone else. This is your life. Live it your way!

## The F-Word

*Fruitful: the purpose of each day*
How often have you heard someone tell you that they were searching for the meaning of life? What is this mysterious mission?

You inherently know that the past is unchangeable and the future is yet to be determined, but you fail to recognize the value of the *moment* you are currently experiencing.

The present moment is all you have. Use it wisely. Make each day unique by cherishing what is happening right now.

Do not waste your life on could-have-beens or what-ifs! Take control of your life by defining what would make each moment the most fruitful for you. Throw yourself into life with unlimited passion and enthusiasm to avoid the regrets of missed opportunities.

Consider each day fruitful if you *learn, teach,* and *care.*

## Timeless Wisdom

*It is easy to be a harsh critic but often difficult to be a problem-solver.*

Complaining may be entertaining or therapeutic, but it rarely results in a suitable solution. Turn complaints into potential solutions by exploring the root cause of the complaint. Then create a list of potential solutions.

What about …?

*Everything you do defines who you are.*

This is a fundamental truth of the universe. Everything you do on this planet clearly defines who you are. You may veil your true self from others, but you can never fool yourself. You can change who you are by changing your behavior. The longer you procrastinate, the harder it is to change. You are defined by your choices and how you treat others.

A little *self-assessment* is periodically needed to see if who you want to be aligns with who you are being right now.

*To succeed, you have to be comfortable with being uncomfortable.*

For many, the word *comfort* triggers a false sense that there is no need to remain progressive or on the cutting edge. Excuses begin to replace results. The past becomes more important than your present realities.

Comfort can dull your senses, leading to stagnation. This is a major denial of reality. Evolution demands constant change, which can be unnerving for the unprepared.

During my physical after I turned fifty, my doctor told me that I had a very big decision to make. He said at fifty, people decide whether they will begin to eat more and run less. They may decide that their appearance no longer matters. They start to allow their mental capacity to diminish. People become comfortable thinking their most important days are in the past. He challenged me to make my decision.

Live life at full throttle, or casually slow down to a much easier pace. You decide!

# The Cycle of Choice

The great thing about life is your God-given *free will*; the ability to make decisions that you truly believe will benefit your personal goals. Choices make it possible for people to select their own life directions or life journeys. With every decision comes a potential positive or negative result. Outcomes always create responsibility. Responsibility creates more choices. Unfortunately, irresponsibility motivates people to act solely on their emotional self-interest; often unaware of the impact they have on others. Every experience you have ever had was the result of your choices.

---

*But until a person can say deeply and honestly, "I am what I am today because of the choices I made yesterday," that person cannot say, "I choose otherwise."*
—Stephen R. Covey, *The 7 Habits of Highly Effective People: Powerful Lessons in Personal Change*

---

Let's use an example to show the *cycle of choice*.

## Story: The Buying Blues

My wife and I recently discussed purchasing an SUV for shuttling our grandchildren to various events.

Once we decided it was time for a change in vehicles, I asked my wife to go online to research the options she wanted and then narrow her choices to just two vehicles. She eagerly started her in-depth research. With each new vehicle she viewed, she found new features that she liked, which caused her to compare them with other potential selections. Her research went on for days. When I asked her for the two choices, she broke into tears, frustrated that she could not narrow it down to just two. She wanted to look at six different vehicles, which got limited support from me. As with many other similar decisions, we did nothing.

Let's take a moment to review the cycle of choice:

- The first choice was to begin the purchasing process.
- The second choice was to look at SUVs because this type of vehicle was perfect for transporting our five grandchildren to every youthful activity known to man.

These choices were made easily.

Then the trouble started. My wife focused on so many features that all of the vehicles started looking the same. Things that were of limited importance began to fog the process. She liked the color of blue from one manufacturer while preferring the modern GPS system of another. The process that started with enthusiasm became a burden of issues, creating more confusion than clarity.

I had pressed her to narrow it down to only two choices, which caused her considerable stress mixed with a little anger. I quietly retreated from the conversation.

How did this simple task become so complicated?

The first error was seeking and getting bogged down in excessive amounts of detail. In looking at a multitude of vehicles, she had created a strong *fear of choosing*. She feared making a bad choice, so she procrastinated and made no decision.

Lesson learned: when given too many choices, we often feel uncomfortable making any decision.

Our attempt to purchase a new automobile caused tension in our relationship, accompanied by a prolonged process of fact-finding, negotiating, and comparison.

When I shared this frustrating experience with friends, they echoed similar experiences.

We all make choices constantly. This example involved a vehicle purchase, but some of your choice challenges are much greater in severity and consequence.

---

*In any moment of decision, the best thing you can do is the right thing. The worst thing you can do is nothing.*

—Theodore Roosevelt

---

For you to make choices, you must have confidence in your ability to make the best choice under the present circumstances. If you lack this confidence, you will shy away from decision making. This makes you a potential servant to the decisions of others.

So how can the process be improved or simplified to effectively lead to a positive conclusion?

## Ten Rules for Making Good Choices

### *Rule 1: Do Not Over Research Your Options*
Being paralyzed by information overload or too many priorities is very common. You complicate your life by second-guessing what you feel. You may work under the very inaccurate assumption that more information leads to a far better decision. Often, more information leads to either no real decision or a choice made out of frustration.

---

*Desires dictate our priorities, priorities shape our choices, and choices determine our actions.*

—Dallin H. Oaks

---

### *Rule 2: Narrow Your Options to Two*
This allows you to truly compare each based on the same criteria. This will let you see the very best option for you. Too many options create confusion. A choice between two options should ease the process.

*Rule 3: Never Make a Decision Without Proper Reflection*

Rash decisions lead to choices made on emotion and emotion only. Impulse decision making is risky and expensive. All decisions create an intentional or unintentional consequence. Hasty decisions made during emotionally charged situations often bring regret.

*Contemplation is the highest form of activity.*

−Aristotle

*Rule 4: Have a Specific and Designated Place Where You Make Decisions*

I suggest that you always make your decisions behind your desk at home or at work. People may often catch you off guard after a meeting or when you are focused on another issue. *Cause a pause* to allow time for you to think more thoroughly about your decision. A decision is made not just with emotion but with emotion balanced by rational thinking. When appropriate, have other decision makers join you.

*Rule 5: Identify Nonnegotiable Choice-Eliminating Issues that Need to Be Considered*

A *choice eliminator* is an element that is so important, it literally cannot be overlooked. Choice eliminators demand another option.

For example, Sue meets a man and falls in love. She wants a lifetime commitment, which includes marriage and children. Ron, her lover, already has children from his first marriage. He really wants to marry Sue, but he is very firm about not having any more kids. Children are the *choice eliminator* making marriage to Ron impossible.

*The right choice is hardly ever the easy choice.*

−Rick Riordan, *The Throne of Fire*

*Rule 6: Consider Every Stakeholder Impacted by Your Choice*

Has adequate consideration been given to the desires, feelings, and preferences of all the people who will be directly and immediately impacted by the outcome?

Open discussion with potential stakeholders allows for input rather than unilateral announcements. Show each involved person how the choice will personally impact him or her. Consensus must be achieved prior to the determination of a decision. Consensus after the announcement of a decision is highly improbable. The decision will likely be seen as a dictate or, worse still, a mandate.

*Rule 7: Limit the Amount of Time Needed to Make Your Decision*
Without a specific timeline, people tend to procrastinate or lose focus. This often may lead you to blame external conditions for failing to make a choice.

---

*An excuse is worse and more terrible than a lie.*

−Alexander Pope

---

You have many things to decide daily. Without a specific deadline, an important decision can be delayed, missed, or forgotten.

For example, Samuel has been married to June, his second wife, for about three years. Samuel knew he needed to change the beneficiary on his life policies to June, but he just never took the time to handle the paperwork. Sam went to work but unfortunately was killed in a car accident on his way home. Because of his procrastination, the proceeds of his life insurance policies went to his first wife, Margaret, rather than to June.

*Rule 8: Once Your Decision Has Been Made, Take Immediate Action*
A decision made needs no further reflection.

Avoid the after-the-fact input of others. All additional information will do is cause you to doubt your decision. Do not set yourself up for the emotional roller-coaster ride caused by reconsideration.

---

*There are three constants in life... change, choice and principles.*

−Steven Covey

---

*Rule 9: Rejoice When a Decision Is Made*
Making decisions is very difficult, so *celebrate* your courage to make a choice.

### Rule 10: Understand that Making Decisions is Difficult

It is hard for people to make decisions. Help them learn these simple rules.

It is very challenging to be faced with so many possible alternatives. It is very important to develop a personal *moral compass* that creates uncompromising standards that will direct your life. Your real *moral compass* is the by-product of family, society, close friends, social norms, and your personal experiences.

Without consistent standards to guide your way, you may have difficulty making a sound choice that leads to a positive consequence.

Many people have no standards to guide their way. This generally leads to very poor choices with very negative or catastrophic consequences.

Decision making is a learned skill. Take full command of your life by choosing wisely.

---

*Choose your love. Love your choice.*

–Thomas S. Monson

---

# The F-Word

### Free: the God-given right of choice

In every circumstance, each person has the right, given by God, to make his or her personal choice. What makes you unique is the background and experience you bring to the process.

A classic choice made by individuals on a regular basis is called *flight-or-fight.*

When faced with a probable confrontation—emotional, verbal, or physical—you must quickly determine your best option. Should you stand your ground, or is it appropriate to flee?

In either case, your actions will be observed and judged by others, who are using their own right or wrong matrix. Thus, it is important that you do not allow the opinions of others to alter your opinion of yourself. Better put, do not let others rent space in your head.

In the final accounting, your choice belongs to you and you alone. You will benefit from your good choices; you will pay the price for your poor ones.

You are the master of your own fate. Do not let anyone make your choices for you. Make your own decisions.

If the choices of others tend to challenge your personal standards, determine how to seek clarity from the other person about the motive of his or her choice. If that motive is self-serving and harmful to you, detach yourself from that person, place, or thing. Don't allow the motives of another person cloud your judgment or your vision of yourself.

The universal law of attraction will always compel you to seek people with whom you have things in common. So select your friends, business associates, and lovers based on your mutual strengths and commonalities.

## Timeless Wisdom

*"Awareness mobilizes… fear paralyzes." (Neal Donald Walsh)*
Awareness gives you a reason for action. Awareness is immediately sizing up the environment around you and then deciding on your appropriate response.

Fear freezes you in your tracks. There is a reason why the victim being chased by the bad guy in a horror movie just screams and awaits the killing blow.

Fear holds you back, while love moves you passionately forward.

*The person who remains calm generally wins.*
In every situation, regardless of the internal turmoil you may be experiencing, always remain calm. No emotional outburst or reaction can defeat being calm. Remaining calm defuses emotion, leading to rational resolutions.

Unwanted things happen to everyone. They often cause a disruption in your life that is unwanted or harmful. You may not be able to control what happens, but you can surely control how you react.

---

*Getting angry is frustration exposed. It indicates that something has happened to you that you do not want or that you are not getting something you truly want.*

—Neale Donald Walsch

---

Your feelings trigger an emotion that is expressed in some form of action. You are in absolute control of what that action will be.

Channeled emotion can be a very effective tool in any attempted communication. The essential words used here are both *channeled* and *controlled*. Highly charged outbursts or rants make the speaker look out of control. Being careless with your words is often the quick way to self-destruct. Be unflappable under trying times or moments of challenge.

A person does not control anything in this world other than his or her reaction to life events.

Calm waters are easy to navigate.

*Great relationships are based on win-win outcomes.*

People will viciously fight to the death to prove they're right. Proving you are right means someone else needs to be wrong. Right versus wrong creates winners and losers. Winners generally rejoice after earning a victory, while losers are embarrassed or driven to the extreme of shame.

In every competition, someone will win and someone will lose. The winners always need to win with dignity and humility while at the same time acknowledging the efforts of their opponents.

Being able to determine whether a situation is truly a competition or a difference of opinion is very important in creating win-win outcomes.

In life, differences can be properly negotiated to create some winning elements for both views and participants. This allows both parties to acquire something of value. So when you find yourself in a difference of opinion with another person, seek to discover a mutually beneficial and suitable outcome.

Everyone appreciates a win.

# Right versus Wrong

It is never an easy task to determine right from wrong, since both change with the social morals of the times.

Being right seems to be the motivation that impassions people to do so many things in life. A person will go to extremes to be right. What people fail to realize is that right is in the eye of the beholder. Your right may very well be my wrong. In reality, we may both be right or both be wrong.

---

*More evil gets done in the name of righteousness than any other way.*
—Glen Cook, *Dreams of Steel*

---

You, and most of the people in our world, judge others through your own conceptualized prism. You are drawn to people that believe as you do and are repelled by those whose beliefs dramatically differ from yours. This *attraction-rejection impulse* is one of the natural laws of the universe.

Judgment of the behavior of someone else seemingly gives you the permission to condemn, punish, and reject. It also can give you the presumed authority to reward, promote, and acclaim those with whom you agree.

Judgment has created every social ill that mankind has ever known. Judgment stops conversations. Judgment limits relationships and halts progress. Judgment limits opportunities and creates inequality.

> ... *[I]t would be interesting to find out what goes on in that moment when someone looks at you and draws all sorts of conclusions.*
>
> —Malcolm Gladwell

When you say, "We are not on the same page," what you really mean is, "I am not on your page."

You know that it takes compromise to gain consensus. Compromise can only be attained if and when all parties in the discussion suspend judgment (beliefs of right and wrong) in favor of listening to both sides of an issue. Consensus can be achieved if both sides of an issue have been heard, both sides feel respected, and the final outcome reflects benefits for both sides. This leads to a win-win conclusion.

So replace *judgment* (beliefs of right or wrong) with *observation.*

An observation is your perception of a thing. You own it! A judgment is your evaluation of a thing, which you push onto others!

## Observation

- I noticed you were yelling a lot.
- You have some different information on this issue
- I see that you have arrived fifteen minutes late

## Judgment

- Your yelling is out of line. Stop it!
- Your information is wrong.
- Your tardiness has become a problem that needs to be fixed.

## Characteristics of Observations

- Observations are what you saw.
- You own your observations.
- Observations open discussions.
- Observations give the other person clarity on your position.
- They can often be tolerated within a relationship.

## Characteristics of Judgments

- Judgments are what you felt.
- You project your judgment onto others.
- Judgments are generally met with resistance.
- Judgments create disagreements, debates, and potential hostility.
- They often lead to the end of the relationship.

## Stereotypes Involving Observations and Judgments

- People making observations are open-minded and reasonable.
- People making judgments are self-centered and opinionated.

---

*Good judgment comes from experience, and experience—well, that comes from poor judgment.*

—A.A. Milne,

---

## Story: The Frustrated Grocer

A local grocer experienced several unique discoveries in a single day. Store manager, Frank Sloan, started his day as usual, monitoring the workers in his supermarket. He was so busy that he often did not see the activities that were causing the store to lose money. He decided to spend an entire day looking for ways to improve the store's profit margin.

The first incident of the day was easily observed in the produce department. He realized that it had become a common practice for shoppers to sample the red grapes before making a purchase. In several situations, regular shoppers would do more than just sample the fruit; they would actually take a generous handful of grapes for an early shopping snack. Frank immediately spoke with Joe, the produce manager, about the situation. Joe said he had not wanted to confront the shoppers because he feared the store would lose business if he angered them.

Frank and Joe decided that they would measure how much of a loss the store was taking because of this accepted practice. They were shocked when they discovered that approximately twelve pounds of grapes were being consumed daily at a cost of three dollars per pound.

Frank continued his journey through the store. He noticed another very common practice perpetrated by parents being heckled by crying and irritable children. When a child would act up, a parent would open a small bag of chips or cookies to quiet him or her. The parent would then throw the empty bag onto one of the shelves to avoid having to pay.

Things settled down for a while, until Frank observed a fifty-year-old man shove a loaf of bread under his jacket and attempt to leave the store without paying. Clancy, the security guard, apprehended him on the sidewalk in front of the store.

When Clancy questioned the man, he was told that the man had no job, no money, and several hungry children to feed. He knew he was stealing, but he considered it necessary to feed his kids.

Frank went on with his search. He noticed a disturbing action by his butcher in the meat department. The butcher would put his thumb on the scale when weighing most of the premium meats. He was very careful not to be noticed by the customers. His department was one of the highest profit segments of the store.

Finally, Frank had his last encounter for the day. In the late afternoon, a group of twelve- and thirteen-year-old boys wandered into the store. They were very loud and distracting. This was a diversionary tactic that allowed one of the younger boys to grab several items from a shelf and stuff them into his jacket. He signaled to his pals that the deed had been done. They all quickly left the store. Clancy actually witnessed the entire shoplifting crime. He apprehended the young thief and one of his friends.

When Tommy, the young shoplifter, confessed under questioning from Clancy, he shared that he had stolen the goods as an initiation prank to get into a gang at his middle school. He said he was sorry and hoped the store would let him go because it was just a stupid prank.

Frank was exhausted when he got home. His wife, Betty, listened to the description of his day.

"Today, I decided to spend a part of my day observing the activities in the store to identify areas where I could make the store more profitable and efficient. What I saw was shocking!

"First, I saw how many people felt free to eat a sample of the grapes. My goodness, one lady consumed probably a half a pound of red grapes before she left the produce department. Then I saw several moms give their kids chips or cookies to keep them quiet. Of course they never paid for the items.

"The customers don't understand that all of our losses force us to increase the prices of staple products like milk, bread, and eggs! All of the shoppers at the store are being harmed by the actions of a few.

"Joe, our lead butcher, is applying extra weight to the scales when he measures the weight of most meat. The shoppers are paying much more than they should. I don't know how long this has been going on and how big of a problem this really is.

"And there is more! Clancy caught two shoplifters today. One was an older man who claimed he was stealing to feed his starving family, and the other was a twelve-year-old kid from Jefferson Middle School who stole three items as a gang initiation."

What is really right, and what is wrong? There were laws broken in these dramatic examples. There were also numerous breaches in ethical behavior.

Right and wrong is clearly defined by society when a law is violated. Society created the laws to protect the innocent owners and customers from blatant violations by individuals who would rob them of their dignity, possessions, and safety. Should we now consider the reasons or motives of instigators when society passes judgment on these individuals to determine their punishment? Whatever we do or don't do will set the tone for future activities and outcomes. By confronting unethical shoppers, will the store lose their business? What might happen to store profits if the meat department changes its practices? Should the butcher be fired for his actions, even though he did it to make the store more profitable? Should the adult be charged with shoplifting, regardless of his desperation? Should the thieving kid get off the hook because he was pressured to steal?

Finally, now that Frank knows the truth, what should he do? What are the consequences of taking or failing to take action? Does Frank become a knowing accomplice by allowing things to remain according to the status quo?

Should he view the grape snatchers differently than the butcher, the teen thief-seeking acceptance differently than the man trying to feed his family? They all took something that did not belong to them and harmed the storeowner and customers in the process. Do their reasons change the harm or the loss?

---

*There is no wrong time to do the right thing.*
—Charles M. Blow

---

Each of us wrestles with this kind of dilemma every day. When you face your expected or unexpected challenges, do you revert to *situational ethics*— ethics based on the offense and motive of the offender—rather than your true belief of right or wrong? When you go outside your personal standards of right and wrong, you are subjected to the judgment of others, who, because of varying elements, see life in a different way. The best method of coping with these differences is to suspend judgment until you fully understand the facts. Seek to sincerely understand both sides before labeling the offense or the offender.

Once all the information is completely ascertained, you are prepared to make a decision. More importantly, you will have to decide how you will manage your reaction and your emotions.

Always choose your battles wisely. You cannot be a contributing and responsible member of society or mankind if you do not hold true to your values.

Don't rush to a fight. Moving quickly may rob you of the chance to fully understand all aspects of a situation.

---

*Love all, trust a few, do wrong to none.*
—William Shakespeare, *All's Well that Ends Well*

---

No matter what specific decision you make, it will incur criticism from someone. You will hear all kinds of reasoning:

- Let the kid off this time. It is his first time. He never would have stolen without the peer pressure to belong.
- The man was just stealing the bread to feed his family. I would do the same thing if I had to. Be charitable and just give him the bread.

- Do not risk losing a customer who spends hundreds of dollars a month in your store over a few lousy grapes or some cheap kiddy treats. See the big picture.
- Do not fire the butcher. He was just trying to help the store. He was simply helping to recover the store losses caused by the customers.

Sadly, compromising your ethical beliefs and standards, if discovered, will be seen as a flaw in your character, even though your actions were really intended to show compassion.

---

*Your behaviors are supported by your thinking patterns.*
—Dr. Wayne W. Dyer,
*How to Change Lifelong Self-Defeating Thinking Habits*

---

You should never compromise yourself to protect the actions of another. Each time you do, you weaken your moral resolve, as well as your personal identity.

Here is a *huge truth*: Absolutely everything you say and every action you take define who you are! Your actions and words also define who you will become and how others will see you.

The simple truth is that once you allow your emotions to dominate over your common sense, you have entered the danger zone. Raw emotions are the common denominator in every mistake you have ever made. It is the joining of your passion with common sense that helps you make prudent, well-thought-out decisions. Fight the instinct to simply react. Replace reacting with a willingness to learn and understand.

For every action there is always a reaction. No action is without consequence. In the examples observed by Frank, you saw several cases of people behaving in a manner that goes against society's collective moral code. Each person—the shopper, the butcher, the young teen, and the parent—acted outside the parameters of acceptable behavior. They broke the law that was created for the mutual benefit of everyone. Shoppers do not want to pay more for their products because of the malicious acts of others. They also want to get what they pay for, which makes the actions of the butcher inappropriate.

These intentional perpetrators had their own methods of rationalizing their actions to justify their behavior. All of their motives are very different. The grape snatcher is only a selective consumer. The butcher is helping his store remain profitable. The teen is being young and stupid. Finally, the shoplifting parent was simply trying to feed his family. Is any one explanation more valid than the other? Should you be more sympathetic to the parent than to the teen because of the motives behind the act? Is the loss of value any different to the harmed shoppers based on the actions of the grape snatcher or the unethical butcher? If you measure all the behaviors against the achieved outcome, no motive or rationalization makes one of these acts less harmful than another.

---

*Decide to begin choosing instead of excusing*
—Dr. Wayne W. Dyer, *How to Change Lifelong Self-Defeating Thinking Habits*

---

## The F-Word

*Faith: the ability to believe in something or someone despite challenges and hardships*

Faith is your ability to believe in something or someone despite challenges to the contrary. It requires a sound personal moral compass founded and grounded on your personally designed *fundamental standards.*

Faith comes from planned *preparation and anticipation.* Winners are confident that they have done the needed preparation to be successful. They anticipate success as the natural outcome of their focus, determination, and hard work. They are very confident in their ability and adaptability. They prepare for each possibility, knowing the right action will be taken for each opportunity. They have faith in themselves.

Self-doubt and negativity, on the other hand, can erode faith. These two mindsets can strip the best person of his or her ability to accomplish a goal. Confidence, not unsupported arrogance, will always win the day.

Faith is the acceptance of the moment, knowing that its clarity of purpose will be known in the future. Each moment or experience will play its small part in one's life journey.

Faith allows individuals to rise above tragedy and seek something positive from each experience.

Winners get knocked down often but never consider remaining down. They lift themselves up! Each stumble is used as a learning tool for grander results in the future.

Winners are admired for their consistent determination and commitment. Losers are easily recognized by their excuses and bad choices.

## Timeless Wisdom

*Always do the right thing, at the right time, for all the right reasons.*

This is literally a mantra for a life well lived. Doing the right thing is often difficult. Its difficulty does not alter what is right! Doing the wrong thing will never be right for you!

The timing of your right action or spoken word may be critically important. Choose your time to be right.

Finally, always do the right thing for the correct reason. Your motive will determine whether something was accidental or intentional.

Your right may not be right for everyone.

*Judgment breeds confrontation, which can make even a good message meaningless.*

When you judge another person, you pass your opinions or attitudes on to them. They may have a very different vision of life. Refrain from judging!

Messages that judge others leave little middle ground for compromise. Excessive judgment excludes people in a time when the world encourages diversity.

Make your message meaningful to everyone.

Do not judge. *Observe* instead.

*Common sense is not so common anymore!*

Common sense is giving thoughtful consideration to any action, tempered with moderation. The question must be, "What would a prudent person do right now?"

Rash actions or words are always part of the formula that leads to catastrophe. Common sense is reflection before action. It is also necessary to determine the best action to take.

Today many people say and do anything they want and then act surprised when it backfires on them. The only thing in life you truly control is your reaction to life's experiences. Common sense balances emotion and logic.

# The Skill of Persuasion

Most of us do not like working with salespeople. Really? Take a moment to reflect on this statement. Do you realize that we are all in sales? The plumber sells his or her ability to fix your pipes, a teacher sells his or her ability to explain complex ideas, and the fireman sells his or her ability to save lives. In other words, each of us has to market and sell our skills, talent, and products in order to receive compensation.

## Exercise

## Activity

Take one minute to write down the skills, talent, or products you have to sell for compensation.

_____

_____

_____

_____

_____

_____

_____

What is the future of your skills, talent, and products in the global market of today?

_____

_____

Would you ever apply your skills, talent, and products without compensation? Of course not! Your personal compensation or economic worth is dependent on what you have to offer against the need of others for your services or products.

*A life isn't significant except for its impact on other lives.*
—Jackie Robinson

We all employ the *skill of persuasion* to help others believe they need what we have to offer. The following are some very important and valuable dos and don'ts about the *skills of persuasion*.

## The Skill of Persuasion

*Don'ts*

- Telling people what they need never works.
- Logic is always a good ally, but rationality alone will rarely bring another person to a different view.
- Emotionally charged pleas without a correspondingly engaging story or example are often rejected.
- Threatening or scaring people has a short-term impact.
- Judging another's behavior as wrong will cause minds to close, followed by either pushback or a lack of support.
- Interrogating a person with yes-or-no questions sets a trap for the person being questioned.
- Never personalize your opinion or criticism of the other person.
- Avoid public confrontations; they lead to bruised egos and embarrassment.
- Do not share the contents of your personal discussion with others. Confidentiality is a critical element of any true relationship.

- Do not attempt to score a win. If you win, that means someone else has to lose. (Strive for a win-win solution.)
- Do not bring past indiscretions into the conversation.
- Do not speak in "I" sentence formats.
- Do not challenge the feelings of the person with whom you are talking. It will frustrate him or her and end the conversation.
- Do not presume the attitude of the person you wish to influence or the outcome of the conversation.
- Do not talk too much.

*Dos*

- You must change a person's belief before he or she will change his or her behavior.
- A person needs to be disturbed before he or she will make a change. The deciding element of any change is based on how that person feels rather than how he or she thinks.
- The emotional impact of a story or example makes the information real. It allows your conversation partner to relate to the illustration.
- After creating an issue via an engaging story, always offer to assist the listener to find a potential and viable solution.
- Listen to the ideas of another before moving to a solution. It is essential to show respect for the other person's point of view. Develop a collaborative bridge that will lead to a mutually acceptable outcome.
- View each conversation as a respectful exchange of thoughts. Remain calm.
- Remain global or general with your comments or criticisms. Personalized attacks simply create resistance to new thoughts.
- Sensitive issues should be discussed in private.
- A meaningful discussion is based on trust. The quickest way to lose trust is by sharing the private contents of a conversation outside of the intended participants. Keep the comments and content of your conversation partner confidential.
- Seek win-win outcomes obtained through influencing.
- Focus on the present and the future, not the past.

- Use examples or your life experiences to create easy-to-understand analogies for the listener.
- Seek engagement and information through the skill of asking open-ended questions. Get the other person(s) talking.
- Remain inquisitive rather than judgmental.
- Suppress your judgment. Realize the power of silence.
- The *skill of persuasion* requires a great deal of practice. To influence the opinion of another person, you must help to identify the prevailing myths and replace them with information, knowledge, experience, and emotional intelligence.

## Tools of Influence

When a conversation goes to an objection, pushback, or stalls, use these three *f*'s to keep it alive:

1. I know how you *feel*.
2. I *felt* that way myself.
3. I *found* … [insert discovery].

*Feel* conveys empathy. *Felt* bonds through mutual experience. *Found* replaces fears with positive options, alternatives, and consequences.

## Using the Three *F*'s

*Sales Presentation*

Prospect: "I appreciate everything you said about protecting my family against catastrophic problems like car accidents or having a house fire, but I see no need to discuss my life insurance plan with you."

Salesperson's response: "Mr. Smith, I know how you *feel*. This is a subject that makes many people uncomfortable. I *felt* the same way when I was approached on the same topic. I *found*, however, that by listening to information about potential protection plans, the cost of buying life insurance was easily adjustable to my budget limitations. We actually have a plan that can fit any budget. Could I quickly show you something that really helped a client of mine who is very much like you?"

People never want to be sold; they want to be educated, which means experiencing a very open and candid conversation that turns myths into knowledge. They want to understand the urgency of an issue or problem. They want to get a personally tailored solution.

*Loyalty publicly results in leverage privately.*

—Andy Stanley

Once again, let us use examples.

Meaningful, honest, and specific conversations can save lives and often prevent a catastrophe. Honesty is what we all deserve to give and receive, so don't confuse influence and honesty. Influence is the style you use to be honest.

*You don't have to be a person of influence to be influential. In fact, the most influential people in my life are probably not even aware of the things they've taught me.*

—Scott Adams

*Doctor's Appointment*

Your doctor tells you that the mole he spotted during your recent exam has him concerned. He wants to remove the mole before you leave his office and order a lab analysis for cancer.

You had been ignoring the growing mole for months, hoping it would simply go away on its own. Your doctor has now alerted you to the possibility of cancer and wants to remove the current mole to prevent further growth and order lab work to determine exactly what additional action will be necessary.

The doctor says, "I realize you may *feel* nervous about my comments and the need for additional testing. I *felt* the same thing when I had additional testing on a medical problem. I *found* that I really had a minor issue that could be treated without any major surgery. I think you will find that this is not a serious problem."

*Mom's Broken Hip*

You have to take your seventy-five-year-old mother to an assisted care facility because she broke her hip when she fell in her kitchen. She lives alone and relies heavily on you for her needs. While in the care facility, the staff determines that your mother also has a form of Alzheimer's disease. They advise you that she can no longer be left alone.

The medical advisor says, "I know how you *feel* about this new diagnosis. I *felt* the same way when I received similar news about my father. I *found*, however, that there are many things an assisted care facility could do to help both me and my parent. Let's set up an appointment with the on-site counselor to explore options for your mom."

The *feel, felt, found* method helps the listener to accept the emotion that accompanies the moment, creates empathy toward the situation, and creates hope by tactfully moving a person toward potential solutions.

---

*You can't make a difference unless you are different.*

—Chris Hodges

---

# You Persuading You

It is a universal truth that what you think becomes your reality. This leads to a very important conclusion. You must be very cautious of how you persuade yourself.

Your confidence and willingness to take action is a direct reflection of how you view yourself. Believing in your own abilities will encourage you to take action. Doubting yourself can often lead to inaction, delays, and, in some cases, procrastination.

What you believe is a form of personal persuasion. You literally make a clear mental decision that your body is compelled to follow. Even if the body and soul do not agree with your commanding thought, your mind has programed your behavior, supporting your defined mental decision. Since your mind may be in conflict with your body and soul, you can experience confusion, anxiety, and stress.

How you persuade yourself or program your mindset will directly determine your professional and personal life results.

*Clouds cannot cover secret places, nor denials conceal truth.*
—Demosthenes

## Denial and Procrastination

In a conversation with a general practice physician, I asked, "Tell me, what is the most serious disease that we currently face in the United States?" His answer was immediate and surprising: "Procrastination!"

He went on to say that at least once or twice a week a patient comes to him with a medical condition that has existed for some time but that has been ignored. By the time the doctor is consulted, many of these conditions, which could have potentially been resolved through early diagnosis, need the attention of a specialist. And some are simply beyond any beneficial treatment.

That leads to a brief but important discussion on why people procrastinate.

There is no one among us who does not procrastinate on a daily basis. We often put things off even though we know that delaying action normally intensifies the issue. Thus, a small problem becomes a catastrophe.

It often reverts back to the *pain-pleasure reality*. You naturally try to avoid pain and seek pleasure. If you can experience pleasure now, you will opt for that outcome, even if the future will be negatively impacted by your decision.

You eat that strawberry pie *a la mode* after dinner because you enjoy the taste, but you seriously lament that decision when it comes time to go bikini shopping.

You indulge your overwhelming need for nicotine by smoking a cigarette but ignore the death warning on the side of each package.

My mother's entire family smoked. Each relative died of lung cancer. None of them were willing to suffer the discomfort of quitting. My dear old dad decided to quit in his early fifties, which extended his life. He passed away at ninety-three years old.

My conclusion was simple: do not start smoking. By watching my relatives' behavior, their addiction, and their subsequent troubles, I clearly saw the damage caused by smoking. I wisely opted to remain a nonsmoker on my march to equal my father's long life span.

How often are teens talked into doing things that they would not normally do, all to avoid peer pressure or prevent a confrontation? To avoid the pain of not going along with the crowd, they experience the pleasure of being accepted by their friends.

What about a cheerleading squad that went to Southern California for a competition? To make the trip a tad bit more enjoyable, the entire squad was treated to one day at Disneyland. While at Disneyland, some of the cheerleaders decided to shoplift small items out of the park's stores. They pressured others in the group to do the same. The Disney security team caught the guilty girls. The police were contacted, the parents were immediately informed, and the information was reported in the local newspaper. More than a dozen cheerleaders were suspended from the squad. Luckily, some team members resisted the peer-pressured thefts. They were, however, harmed by the negative press and impact on the squad's performance that year.

These young women came from an affluent community. They did not need the items they stole. Their actions made them feel daring and naughty and served as an act of passage into the popular crowd.

---

*There's one advantage to being 102. There's no peer pressure.*
—Dennis Wolfberg, *Humorous Quotes for All Occasions*

---

Procrastination is based on the believed perception that a person can ignore the obvious while still realizing a positive outcome. They deny that a problem or situation exists to avoid the negative consequences of moving toward a solution.

Denial is replaced by reality when you put on your trusty and loyal pair of jeans only to realize they have not gotten smaller but apparently you have become larger. One course of action is to go out and buy a larger size. The other solution might be a commitment to going to the gym every other day for an hour workout.

It is natural that we do not want to deny ourselves some of the things we love:

- dessert after dinner
- beers with the guys

- watching TV
- chocolate
- ice cream
- fast food

With a little moderation today, you guarantee a brighter tomorrow. Bad habits are called bad for a reason. They have undesirable consequences that cannot be blamed on anyone other than you.

You create your own life experience. You determine what you will do, who you will be, and where you are going with your life. Everything you do is a defining statement of who you are. Each choice is a link in the chain of your life, leading to exactly where you are today.

So if you want to influence others, start practicing on yourself first.

Be aware that *skillful persuading* can't replace honesty.

---

*The way a message is delivered, is the message.*
—Bryant McGill, *Simple Reminders: Inspiration for Living Your Best Life*

---

## Awareness

Before starting such a conversation, establish your true interest in the well-being of your conversation partner. Then realize you need to help that very person become aware of his or her behavior.

## Observing versus Judging

Make sure you simply express what you observe. When you judge another's behavior, you're making a moral assessment of the other person. You have defined right and wrong based on your personal value system. Your values will often disagree with the values of others. Judgment ends conversations. It breeds confrontation. Judgment is often perceived as arrogant, which makes the message meaningless.

## Self-Expression

Once the observation is made, it is very important to get the reaction of the person observed. Simply ask if your observation was what the sender intended.

## Benefits and Consequences

Explore the benefits and consequences of the observed behavior. Ask questions to open up the dialogue while soliciting the comments of the other person or persons.

## Avoid Trying to Fix

You have not been asked for your observation or to fix the person you have observed based on your point of view or your values. People can only fix themselves. They must decide both when and how. Listen rather than talk.

## How Can I Help?

Summarize the key observations that resonate with your friend. Share with your friend the personal values you heard him or her express.

For example, you could say: "You candidly admitted that you have been very short tempered and quick to snap while closed to the new ideas of others. You are a genuinely kind person who loves being with others. You like to laugh, finding the lighter side of most situations. Your behavior does not seem to be supporting what you value. Do you agree with my observations? Do you want to do something about this? How can I help?"

Always remember, the secret to influencing others is to replace judgment with observations.

## Set a Follow-Up

Regardless of your friend's willingness to make a change or to receive help, arrange a future contact to check in. He or she may need a little time to reflect on the content of the discussion.

## Do Not Push; Gently Pull Instead

*Pushing* is symbolized by someone's hand on your back, forcing you to go in the specific direction in which they want you to go. The mere fact that you are being pushed indicates reluctance on your part.

When you *pull* someone, you are seen as assisting and supporting him or her. You are sincerely moving that person to the finish line.

*Pushing* can appear to be self-serving or insensitive to the needs and feelings of the other person. It implies that you have already set a goal of change and a timeline for your friend without his or her agreement.

*Pulling* comes from a position of caring. Generally, to pull someone, you must be actively engaged in the same endeavor. You are often leading by example. It employs the skill of influencing or persuading rather than telling. It demonstrates your willingness to collaborate rather than to force, direct, or insist.

## The F-Word

*Feelings: the emotions that make us human*

You are a person who has been molded and influenced by your personal life experiences, what you have been taught, and what you have observed. This makes you gloriously unique. Rejoice in your true uniqueness for it makes you stand apart from any other.

Your background, faith, teaching, and observations also develop into what you affectionately call your feelings. They become your sixth sense in all you experience. They help you define who you want to be. They help create your personal life mission, a purpose, and what you believe to be true.

Feelings are real. They are the messages sent to your mind from your soul. They should neither be denied nor ignored.

Your feelings are the birthplace of your emotions. How you feel will determine your physical and psychological balance. Emotions follow your feelings. They're the true manifestation of your feelings in real physical or mental form. Emotions demonstrate how you truly feel. Your emotions send a message to all those around you about how you feel or how you might be approached.

Your emotions will either attract or deflect people from wanting to be with you. If you are happy, confident, and pleasant, people are drawn to you. They want to share in your good nature.

When you are mad, detached, or burdened by worrisome thoughts, you repel others. They sense your tattered state of being, which causes them to avoid you for fear that they will also be drawn into some form of negativity.

The question that you must repeatedly ask yourself is what emotion are you projecting outward right now. Is it endearing or isolating? Assess your feelings and your emotions periodically to make sure they are sending the message that you desire to others.

## Timeless Wisdom

*You never have to apologize for what you do not say.*
Who among us does not wish that they could take back something they have said? Many an ill-spoken word has destroyed relationships, started wars, and destroyed reputations.

Idle conversation about others, such as the unbridled spreading of rumors or openly criticizing the behavior of others, can damage their reputation while harming your personal credibility.

Holding your tongue is often a prudent strategy. What you are thinking can remain private if prudent silence is employed. Restrain your words to retain and maintain control. Expressing a feeling or opinion may not often be the wisest tactic.

Silence is golden!

*Bringing out the best in others will bring out the best in you.*
Doing good things makes you feel fulfilled! When you are doing good things, you are at your very best. You have declared who you want to be while demonstrating the pride you feel when helping others.

---

*Never resist a generous impulse.*

—*Mike Flowers*

---

*Humor breaks all tension and generally defuses volatile moments.*
It is very hard to be mad if you are laughing or smiling. Humor is the great mood equalizer. People will want to spend time with you if you make them laugh.

See life through the eyes of a child!

Many women think humor is one of the most important attributes needed in a potential mate.

People who are humorous are fun to be with, take life a little less seriously, and can find life's wonderment in common occurrences.

# Eliminating Soft Words

Your success must be announced for all to hear. Your declaration of intent focuses your vision on only the things that will fulfill your commitment. Define your goal and then willingly share it with others. Use words and actions that definitively state what you intend to do. *Eliminate vague words, shallow covenants, trepidations, and restricted preparation.*

Most importantly, eliminate soft words!

*Story: The Great Race*

The coach came to his best runner and requested that he exceed his best time in his mile run to help the track team win the team competition at the championship meet.

The star said, "I will do my best time ever, Coach. You can count on me!"

The runner did exactly what he said he would do, his best time. Unfortunately, even though he gave his all, the star runner from another team beat that time by less than one second.

Both the coach and the runner were disappointed by the outcome but not with the effort. As the runner sat with his head in his hands, holding back tears, the coach approached him, supported by the rest of the team.

The coach said, "Tim, the team and I want to personally thank you for running your fastest time ever. You did your best, which is all we could ask of you."

Tim looked up, eyes now full of tears, and said, "I let all of you down. I lost the race!"

The track team captain stepped forward to speak. "Tim, you're a champ to me and to all of these other guys. Coach asked for your help. You made a commitment to do your very best and you delivered. There is never any *shame or blame* in giving everything you've got. I am personally proud of being on the same team as you." He moved over to Tim and shook his hand, saying, "Because of you, the entire team has committed to working even harder next season to be the league champions." Each team member gave Tim a handshake, a hug, or a chest bump.

The race will fade in Tim's memory, but he will never forget the reaction of his team and coach.

---

*He that is good for making excuses is seldom good for anything else.*
—*Benjamin Franklin*

---

Tim's success and leadership came from the following actions:

- making a verbal and personal commitment to excel
- believing he could meet his commitment
- executing when the race began
- finishing what he started
- emotionally reacting to his results because he really cared about achieving his goal

---

*The best job goes to the person who can get it done without passing the buck or coming back with excuses.*
—*Napoleon Hill*

---

When confronted with a challenge, which is normally several times daily, you get a unique chance to see the character of each person involved. The positive thinkers will see an opportunity rather than a challenge. The optimist will give his or her maximum effort. Those who lean toward the negative will minimize their efforts, hoping to solve the challenge with a limited amount of inconvenience.

If you are unwilling to make a commitment, it signifies that you are not confident that you can achieve the goal or you are not willing to give the goal your maximum effort.

You say you will try, meaning the goal is not important to you; you lack a strong sense of urgency; you are not committed to the goal; or you see no personal benefit or consequence for your results. You have given yourself permission to accept any outcome. The victory will belong to someone else who is willing and able to make the sacrifices needed to be a winner.

## Soft Words or Phrases

- I will try.
- I hope to.
- We'll see.
- I'll do what I can.
- I plan to.

These verbalized terms project extremely limited and improbable outcomes. A person who has doubts (fear) is unlikely to succeed.

---

*I attribute my success to this: I never gave or took an excuse.*
—Florence Nightingale

---

## Winning Phrases

- I will.
- I can.
- You can count on me.
- I'll do it.
- I promise.

These terms show grit, commitment, determination, a competitive spirit, and a willingness to do whatever is needed to be successful.

## Example: Calling for Results

To illustrate this concept of soft words, let's look at an example of two telephone solicitors working to make ten appointments. The pressure is on for the end-of-year sales goals. Urgency is the primary motivator, and needed results are the goal. Look at the approaches of each caller.

*Caller 1 Plan*

I will make calls for two hours. I will call from a general list. My reward will be going home.
I will simply call. I will use different ways and approaches. I hope to reach my goal.

*Caller 2 Plan*

I will make calls until I get at least ten appointments. I will call from a screened list of likely prospects. I will reward my success with a nice dinner. I will call and record my results. I will develop a script that I will perfect. I will reach my goal.

Who do you think will probably get the best results? I think it is clear that caller 2 will likely have more immediate, consistent, and productive results.

The name of the success game is *persistent action* on prequalified candidates. Success is the most important single component to building confidence. Confidence is imperative to present anything with enthusiasm and to display the real conviction of undeniable belief in your solution, product, or plan.

---

*Today expect something good to happen to you no matter what occurred yesterday. Realize the past no longer holds you captive. It can only continue to hurt you if you hold on to it. Let the past go. A simply abundant world awaits.*

—Sarah Ban Breathnach,
*Simple Abundance: A Daybook of Comfort and Joy*

---

## The F-Word

*Flexible: the skill of adapting and evolving*

You are a product of your own thinking. Life is not a continuum of consistency. Change is a constant partner. It cannot be avoided, but it can be delayed. Your ability to adapt to the endless changes in life is one of the natural laws of the universe. Those that choose not to adapt do not evolve. They become endangered species, incapable of reinventing themselves to cope with circumstances in the present reality.

The rigidity of your thinking and actions may cause you to be unaccepting of new innovations, new possibilities. This same inflexibility can cause you to become angry about the future; it might even cause you to sink to a level of despair.

Take heart and know that you will be shown the way when the time comes for change. See the possibilities, not the limitations. Rejoice in change for it is a clear sign that you are evolving to a higher level of being.

All things happen at exactly the right time in your life and history. You must learn to become a master of acceptance so you can take advantage of each new opportunity. You are the master of your own fate. That's not to say that you can control all things of the world, but you certainly can determine how you'll choose to deal with them.

Think opportunity and evolve!

## Timeless Wisdom

*Quitting is an addictive disease that generally erodes confidence and creates a timid approach to life.*

Quitting is an act of giving up hope. It disables you. It often causes you to dislike yourself, regretting that you did not see your task through to completion.

Never ever give up.

*Mediocrity does not qualify for a reward.*

You did an average job, so you receive a medal or a trophy. Often, rewards are given out not for exemplary results but for simple participation. This method dampens the natural competitive spirit that resides in all of us.

Your reward for trying is the experience itself. If you desire a medal or a trophy, you must commit to greater *preparation* and more *perspiration*.

You do not get rewarded for showing up!

*The greatest quality a person can have that leads to success is perseverance.*

Do you know anyone who is so driven and determined that they will not ever succumb to failure? They simply cannot surrender; it is not in their nature.

We all love people like this!

Keep on keeping on!

# Rules of Success

I have a very long and loving relationship with the sport of swimming. I was a competitive swimmer since I was a kid, which led me to a very productive coaching career when my personal competitive days came to an end.

Swimming is a rather boring sport, getting up at 5:00 a.m. to go to morning practice, only to return at 3:30 p.m. for a second practice, swimming about four hours a day. No practice was called off because of bad weather. Sunday was the only day of rest.

I will be honest with you: I really didn't like practicing much, lap after lap, over and over. I would hum a song I had no doubt heard on the radio that morning, whether I liked it or not. How fun would it be for you to repeat the lyrics of funky town or a woman singing "let it go, let it go?"

So why did I make such a commitment of time and energy and sacrifice other social activities? I loved to race! Standing on the swimming block, awaiting the starter's gun with my adrenaline soaring was a great high for me. I was swimming against time. I loved pushing my physical strength to the limit.

So why mention this part of my life? It simply reflects the key elements that it takes to be a winner in any and all life endeavors.

## The Key elements of Success

## Commitment

To be a success in any activity, you need to make an irrevocable *commitment* to your goal.

---

*Desire is the key to motivation, but it's determination and commitment to an unrelenting pursuit of your goal—a commitment to excellence—that will enable you to attain the success you seek.*

—Mario Andretti

---

Think of this as the difference between shooting a rifle versus firing a shotgun. The rifle shot does not allow for any error. A shotgun blast is equally as deadly but does not require the same degree of accuracy. Both a rifle shot and that of a shotgun require tremendous focus. Expertise is achieved through repetition, correction, and more repetition. To master any skill, you will need to be totally committed to a specific endeavor.

## Research

Once the goal is defined, it is very important that you invest the appropriate amount of background research so that you can create a plan that will place you in the correct environment to develop your skills.

---

*What we find changes who we become.*

—Peter Morville

---

*Story: The Budding Moviemaker*

A young man always had a fascination about making movies. His parents bought him an inexpensive video camera at a very early age to encourage his interest. He would play with the camera for countless hours each day. Eventually, he announced to his family that he was ready for his first movie premier. Family, neighbors, and friends gathered around the television to witness what they thought would be a short, childish, crude, and simplistic film. As the film began, the crowd was amazed at the quality of the hand-printed titles, the crisp color, and the quality of the editing. The acting was

44

very sincere but amateurish. The story followed a day in the life of a fourth grader. When the five-minute film ended, the audience jumped to their feet with sincere, enthusiastic applause. The producer, director, and main actor took a humble bow.

After researching his options, he selected and purchased a more elaborate camera.

His passion pushed him through various amateur film contests. With each new film, he gained experience as well as confidence in his talent.

He went on to a four-year education majoring in film production and theater arts.

---

*Mentoring is a brain to pick, an ear to listen, and a push in the right direction.*

–John Crosby

---

## Story: Building a Mentor Relationship

A very wise person once said that if you want to become thin, follow a thin person around and eat what and how they eat.

Everyone wants to succeed, but there is no real virtue in starting at the beginning when you can learn from an expert to accelerate your progress.

Did you know that three of the greatest minds in US history formed a study group where they could bounce ideas off of one another? They could take a simple idea and expand it into something remarkable. Thomas Edison, Henry Ford, and Harvey Firestone were great men but became substantially better because of their association with one another.

They realized that many great dreams went unfulfilled because they seemed way too big or highly improbable. Group thinking often finds the "hows" needed to turn a dream into reality.

---

*Life is a succession of lessons which must be lived to be understood.*

–Ralph Waldo Emerson

---

*Story: The Summer Intern*

Each summer, I hired a summer intern to spend three months with my team. He or she was normally a junior or senior in college who was pursuing a future career in business, computer science, or communications. My team only sought and selected individuals who would contribute to our team goals.

In exchange, I spent time with the interns every chance I got, having them experience the many aspects of being a senior sales executive. They observed and participated in our executive decision-making process, associate work, and life issues, as well as conducting sales appointments, experiencing challenging conversations, and learning and using motivational skills, vision development, effective business management methodology, team dynamics, public speaking, etc.

No college course could have ever given them the education that comes from experience.

It also gave the team the ability to refresh our skills and receive valuable input on how their generation viewed life and work.

In other words, both the team and the interns benefited from this mutually collaborative effort. It was a means of passing valuable knowledge on to willing minds. It also made it possible for the interns to bring the team, especially me, new innovative methods to be more effective.

Everyone benefited! It was fun!

Sadly, a limited number of people approach successful leaders seeking mentorship. The single greatest wealth of knowledge we posses in this world consists of the things known by those who have already traveled the path one intends to explore. No amount of money can purchase the wisdom that can be acquired by simply being in the presence of a skilled professional.

Reach out for help! You will find that many people are willing to give you the time you need if you have a sincere desire to learn.

Approach a potential mentor by taking the following steps:

- Express why you selected the prospective mentor.
- Explain what you are attempting to experience.
- Show your willingness to make a firm commitment.

- Share what benefit you can bring to the mentor.
- Declare your willingness to become a mentor to others.

---

*A dream you dream alone is only a dream. A dream you dream together is reality.*

—John Lennon

---

## Dream

Every great idea started as a simple dream, followed by the trial-and-error process needed to find answers that lead to greatness.

Once again, think of the genius Thomas Edison, who was the greatest failure in American history but also holds the record for the largest number of patents held by one individual. He used the process of elimination to rule out what did not work before he moved to his next experimental attempt. He literally experimented to eventually find the answer.

Every great success came first from an idea. That idea or thought, once put into words, made the idea come alive. The idea expanded and morphed into a plan, which led to action.

Dreamers can see the beauty in a simple stone but are sometimes stifled when taking their dream to fruition. If you are not a true dreamer, if you are not creative or innovative, use an open mind to embrace the dreams of others. Do not be a dream killer, for you may block the next great benefit to mankind.

## Examples of Dreams Fulfilled

- Building the Great Wall of China
- Finding the cure for polio
- Winning the War of Independence
- Building the Golden Gate Bridge
- The San Francisco Giants winning the 3 World Series

*You may encounter many defeats, but you must not be defeated. In fact, it may be necessary to encounter the defeats, so you can know who you are, what you can rise from, how you can still come out of it.*

—Maya Angelou

# Failure

You have all heard the expressions: If you do not fail once in a while, you are probably not doing anything. Great treasures were never found by the weak of spirit; they were the bounty of courageous explorers who continued a quest even in the midst of confusion and setbacks.

Failure is one of your greatest teachers. Like Edison, we can learn from each and every failure, as long as we do not surrender to our own negative impulse to simply quit trying. Edison never saw his work on a success or failure basis. His method was rather simple: experiment enough to eliminate the things that do not work.

*Part of the journey in life is slipping and falling along the way; in these times true friends are the ones who pick you up and dust you off.*

—Ken Poirot

## Story: Life as a Competition

The greatest cheers are often not for the victor of a race but for the competitor who struggled to cross the finish line.

Failing to achieve a gold, silver, or bronze medal would be devastating to many great athletes who sacrificed four years of their lives to willingly pursue their dream of Olympic victory.

For others, they come to the games with little chance of medaling. They come to be counted in the world's elite who are skilled enough to be Olympians. They win no medals but they received the experience, memories and the accomplishment of a lifetime.

A greater victory for some than getting first place is the success of finishing.

*Never quit your dream, but learn to cut your losses and quit your plan if it is not working.*

—Ken Poirot

*If you really want to do, be or have anything then first destroy your greatest 'doubt'. The manifestation of your desire is directly proportional to how much you believe.*

—Hina Hashmi,
Your Life a Practical Guide to Happiness Peace Fulfillment

## Positive Attitude

Never succumb to the negative thinkers, for they are going nowhere and they want you as their companion. To justify their own lack of determination or skill, they will be very happy to convince you to join their ranks. They always seek the short cuts. They are the slowest to make a decision and the quickest to quit at the first obstacle.

Positive people draw optimistic people to them. They radiate confidence and generally have the social skills to encourage others to succeed.

Those people you know who take an inordinate amount of time, compounded by volumes of research, to make a decision often have difficulty separating the need for action from doubts. Since they are the slowest to make a decision, they are the quickest to quit on their decisions. The obstacles they encounter reinforce their original reservations.

People who decide quickly are very reluctant to quit when faced with challenges. They are very determined to prove that they made the right decision to move forward.

Decision making is an art form. It can be neither rash nor excessively prolonged. Be sure that the decision maker in your group is strong and is willing to accept the consequences, good or bad, of the decisions made.

## Attributes of Positive People

Here are some important things to remember about being positive:

- Positive people draw people to them.
- Positive people see the possibilities and the benefits.
- Positive people enjoy socializing and being with others.
- Positive people care for others.
- Positive people aggressively search for ways to help.
- Positive people rarely complain.
- Positive people laugh often and find the humor in life.
- Positive people are eager to learn.
- Positive people reach out to others.
- Positive people are confident.
- Positive people are adaptive.
- Positive people see opportunities, not challenges.
- Positive people live longer and have healthier lives.
- Positive people have stronger and longer relationships.

There appears to be no real benefit to being negative. Negativity is spawned from anxiety and fear. It reverses all of the good values mentioned above.

Most negative people are not aware of how they are perceived by others. They often come across to others as over analytical, self-serving, or noncommittal. They believe that finding all of the problems in a situation or another person will prepare them to properly deal with the perceived challenges. This false assumption draws to them the very kind of circumstances and individuals that they do not want.

According to author Israelmore Ayivory, there are seven things negative people will do to you:

1. Demean your value
2. Destroy your image
3. Drive you crazy
4. Dispose your dreams
5. Discredit your imagination

6. Defame your abilities
7. Disbelieve your opinions

I echo Ayivory when he says, "Stay away from negative people!"

# Experiment

Take a poll of several people who know you very well. Ask them to mark whether they perceive you as positive or negative in all of the categories in the following exercise. Ask them to anonymously return the poll to you.

Next, honestly take the poll on yourself and then overlay the poll responses you get from others with your assessment.

Fight your natural instinct to be defensive or to seek to change the opinion of any poll submitter. What do you want to do about the results?

*Positive or Negative Poll*

Name: _____

Describe your general opinion on each category. Check either positive (+) or negative (-) according to your perception of the individual named above as it relates to the stated category.

| Category | Positive (+) | Negative (-) |
|---|---|---|
| Work | _____ | _____ |
| Life | _____ | _____ |
| Relationships | _____ | _____ |
| Future | _____ | _____ |
| Government | _____ | _____ |
| Religion | _____ | _____ |
| Family | _____ | _____ |
| Health | _____ | _____ |
| Finances | _____ | _____ |
| Other | _____ | _____ |

# Responsibility

*Most people do not really want freedom, because freedom involves responsibility, and most people are frightened of responsibility.*
—Sigmund Freud, *Civilization and Its Discontents*

Accept the responsibility for each of your decisions. No one can determine where your life is going except you. Never surrender your decisions to any person, group, institution, or cause. In turn, that means you are completely responsible for your actions as well as your outcomes. Your past, present, and future have and will rely on the decisions you make or fail to make. Excuses fool no one. They are feeble attempts to shift the lack of results onto someone or something other than yourself.

## Story: The Speeding Ticket

A police officer pulled over a speeding car driven by a seventeen-year-old boy. When the officer approached the young driver, he asked if the boy had a reason for driving so fast. The young man gave a breathless answer, saying that he was heading to the local hospital emergency room after receiving an urgent call that his father had been involved in a serious accident.

The experienced officer wanted to give the young driver the benefit of the doubt, but something did not ring true with his story. The officer called the emergency room to ask about the boy's father. He was told that the boy's father had been to the emergency room about ten hours ago with a bump on his head. He had been released about eight hours ago with a few stitches.

The officer told the boy what he knew about his father. The boy finally confessed that he was on his way to see his girlfriend and just had not been paying attention to his speed.

The officer gave the boy a ticket and informed the young man that he would be personally calling his home to share news of the incident and the false story with the boy's father. The officer told the teenager that the call would not have been necessary if he had simply told the truth when asked.

The boy feared facing his father more than the police. His father took his car away for a month, along with the driving privileges he had with other household vehicles. He was grounded from dating and social activities for the entire month as well. He also had to pay for the ticket.

---

*It is wrong and immoral to seek to escape the consequences of one's acts.*

—Mahatma Gandhi

---

## Accountability

Hold yourself and others accountable for what is said and done. Excuse making is the folly of an irresponsible person; it is simply a feeble attempt to disguise any wrongdoing. Great results do not just happen. It takes hard work, a relentless attitude, consistent practice, and execution to achieve the successful completion of your goals.

*Story: Seeking the Truth in Unexpected Places*

One Saturday morning, my daughter cuddled next to me as we bonded by watching the animated version of Alice in Wonderland. Although I was physically present, my mind was searching for a theme I needed for my big speech the following Monday. My daughter noticed my lack of focus, so she said, "Daddy, you're not paying attention." I told her I was watching and hugged her a little harder.

As I refocused on the movie, the answer to my dilemma appeared in the form of a conversation between Alice and the Cheshire Cat. Alice was walking until she hit a fork in the road. She stood there, perplexed as to which road to take. The cat asked Alice where she was trying to go, to which she replied that she did not know. The cat then responded, "Then it really doesn't matter which road is chosen."

You cannot plan your journey if you do not know your destination. Accountability is the equivalent of road signs along your journey to let you know how you are progressing, where you are, and how you need to adjust your actions to stay on course.

---

*The man who moves a mountain begins by carrying away small stones.*

—Confucius

---

## Believe

You will never change your behavior if you do not first change your belief. No change of behavior is sustainable if you do not change what you believe.

Simply trying is a direct signal to the universe that you do not believe that you can accomplish your goal.

### Story: The Runner

One Saturday morning, I went for my traditional long run. It felt great to be out in the fresh air and pushing my endurance. I got caught up in runner's euphoria, so I lost my focus on how far I had gone. My normal long run was about ten miles round-trip. When I stopped, I realized I had already run ten miles, which meant I needed to run ten additional miles to get home. I turned and looked in the direction of my home, using a hill behind my home as my landmark. I had a flash of panic. I was tired, without any money, phone, or way to get assistance.

I had a momentary breech of confidence in my ability to get back home. I had to give myself a quick pep talk to calm down and compose myself. I told myself that I needed to just take one step at a time rather than focusing on the entire task of running the additional ten miles.

Needless to say, I safely made it back home. It also goes without saying that I did a few more things after this incident:

- I took a long nap.
- I decided to always carry money with me.
- I confirmed that I would take personal identification on my next run.
- I vowed that I would tell someone the route that I would take.
- I identified markers along the way to map my route.

## Coachability

This is your ability to be constantly open to constructive criticism, suspend all judgment, and adjust your actions to achieve better results.

*A coach is someone who can give correction without causing resentment.*

—John Wooden

In order for a person to become a good coach, he or she needs to be *coachable*. A coach will be accepted if the following conditions hold true:

- The person being coached believes the coach cares about him or her.
- The coach has the knowledge and experience to help.
- Positive results will come from the coaching session.
- The coach will provide the motivation and discipline.

Great coaches have a lot of strong abilities. They can:

- build character;
- connect the work with the reward;
- believe in those they coach;
- know what they are talking about;
- have the needed experience or expertise;
- build trust relationships;
- display the traits required of those they coach;
- be tough and, at times, brutally honest; and
- turn potential into reality.

Coach is a title you must earn. It is not about buying a play manual, a ball cap, and a whistle. Rather, it is about building trust. It is about seeing and bringing out the potential in a person while instilling key ideals of rules, practice, execution, adjustment, results, and celebration.

---

*Without self-discipline, success is impossible, period.*

—Lou Holtz

---

Coaching establishes standards and demands relentless practice. It is also requires gathering people of diverse thoughts, backgrounds, and motivations into a cohesive group or team with a single vision of purpose.

Coaching is not easy. It demands a sharp eye, excessive attention to detail, analysis skills, homework, learning, motivation, keen analytical skills, cheerleading, a strong character, determination, and an unflappable belief that the best in most people has yet to be realized.

A coach must *walk the talk* and always lead by example. Hypocrisy in this area has undermined some of the best coaches and leaders in the world.

Every person on this planet serves as an active coach to someone. You tremendously influence those you coach!

Your team members will not remember what you said (the exact words) as much as how they felt after you said it.

Coaching is about believing in someone, believing that every person has greatness inside of him or her that's just waiting for a chance to come forward. Whether it is for a brief and fleeting moment or for a lifetime, every person has a gift to share with the world.

Here is a very short list of a few superb coaches of note that understood and captured the true essence of being a great coach:

- John Wooden—college basketball
- Bear Bryant—college football
- Vince Lombardi—professional football
- Bill Walsh—professional football
- Dale Carnegie—personal development
- Billy Graham—morality and kindness
- Casey Stengel—professional baseball
- Mother Teresa—saintly humanitarian
- Pat Summit—women's college basketball

---

*Seek opportunities to show you care. The smallest gestures often make the biggest difference.*

—John Wooden

---

Many great books have been written about each of these people. Take a little time to explore their stories and to absorb some of the greatest motivational styles of our modern times.

Coaching is not just about sports; it is how you help groom people to achieve success in life. Success is not measured by how many ball games you win, how much money you make, or the size of your home. The number of lives you have bettered by your presence will measure your success.

Coaches have an awesome responsibility to encourage people to excel, especially when attempting seemingly impossible acts.

The common person can discover the great potential he or she has within if motivated to surpass expectations and strive for excellence.

A coach sets the goal to success, followed by a plan that will lead there. The very best way to keep your followers focused is to regularly demonstrate success through your actions, words, and discipline.

Some of the greatest coaches in your life may not have won great championships or awards, but they no doubt helped you discover the incredible winner in you. You may remember their words at some point in your life when you tap into their wisdom.

Being a great coach means you truly care about the people you lead. You want them to become good people with solid values, integrity, and appreciation for the ability to compete.

When building and interacting with a team, truly excellent coaches do several important things:

- Expect people to be honorable and truthful
- Demand they do what they say
- Explain the value of meaningful criticism
- Allow creative thinking and innovative ideas
- Maintain that practice and more practice is the key to good results
- See the potential and the best in everyone
- Give everyone the chance to prove his or her ability
- Create a nonthreatening environment
- Display the core value of doing the right things
- Build relationships based on kindness and respect
- Share the importance of the individual roles
- Profess a philosophy of never go down and stay down
- Believe winning is a great experience and losing is a great teacher
- Win with humility and gratitude

---

*People will exceed targets they set themselves.*

—Gordon Dryden

---

I have been a teacher and coach my entire adult life. We all coach someone on a daily basis (children, coworkers, employees, etc.). You cannot be a good coach unless you are coachable. I have also found that it is very important to ask people for their permission to give them a tip or two. Never offer criticism without getting permission from the person you wish to help.

You also have to earn your coaching credentials. To achieve this, there are several things you must do.

First, be credible through real experience, knowledge, and performance. For example, my father gave me his sincere advice on how often I should actually breathe during my swimming competitions. I appreciated his attempt to help me, but as a non-swimmer he had little credibility.

Focus on actions and techniques without criticizing the person. For example, I hear many frustrated parents tell their children, "Johnny, you are a bad boy!" This just is not true. Johnny is not inherently bad. He may have just done a bad thing. Make sure you do not label a person. Focus your attention on the behavior you witnessed.

Offer potential corrective solutions. For example, help Johnny aggressively practice his basketball free throws to gain confidence, experience, and skills.

During high emotions, delay the coaching. For example, after your son strikes out with the bases loaded, it is probably not the time to take him aside to explain how he could do better next time.

Always ask the person you plan to coach exactly what he or she thought went right and what needs to be improved. For example, let's say a salesperson giving a sales presentation displayed a great deal of knowledge but sadly failed to close the sale because of his lack of enthusiasm about the plan. He had a lot of knowledge, but he needed to work on getting the potential client enthusiastically engaged.

And finally, set up the next experience. For example, the expression often used to typify this thought is when you're thrown off a horse, get right back on. Do not allow anyone to *try-fail-quit*. Quitting is a trap. Quitting is a disease that erodes confidence and creates a timid approach to life.

Coaching is not about showing up for every practice. It is not about praising failure or rewarding mediocrity. Coaching is the skill of building trust in those you coach, trust that you want to help them to be their very best. It is not only about loving them whether they win or lose, but also about honesty without false praise to avoid conflict or criticism.

Of all of the people in my life who have coached me—there have been many—I believe my best coach was the one who made me so angry that I wanted to show her she was dead wrong about me. She forced me to take a long hard look at my behavior, my attitude, and my own awareness about my influence over others.

Unwittingly, she did not realize how our confrontation led to my greatest learning experience, setting the stage for a positive shift in my business career.

## Execution

With all of the other components in place, nothing will be accomplished without action. Not ill-planned random actions started and then abandoned but strategic and specific actions that support the successful completion of your goal.

### Story: Building a Gazebo

A beautiful, welcoming backyard needs to be filled with comforts that allow my friends and family to lounge around on a sunny summer afternoon while enjoying my specially prepared barbecued chicken.

After building my gorgeous house, my attention turned to my very next project, a massive gazebo. As with every project, in the beginning, my enthusiasm was very high, so I drew up some crude plans and visited my friendly home improvement store.

With no experience in building a gazebo, I placed myself in the hands of the experts, who I happily found were both willing and able to assist me.

Purchases made, tools brought out of storage, clothes changed to something I was not afraid to ruin, I declared to my skeptical bride that I was ready and able to begin the construction of the greatest and most well-built gazebo in our neighborhood. She wished me luck and then distanced herself from the project.

It goes without saying that every new venture has its moments of doubt, frustration, and learning. The key is to persevere through each stage.

I started with great *enthusiasm* but with very little real experience. As I progressed, my enthusiasm waned. My frustration consumed my lagging energy because of my learning errors and my numerous return trips to the home improvement store.

What began as excitement morphed into dogged-eared *determination*. I was tired and hell-bent on completing the project. My wonderful wife was my key motivator, using assorted sighs, smirks, and impatient glances.

The final day of the project I proudly declared that the gazebo had been constructed, painted, and was finally ready to be unveiled. I planned a barbecue for my family and close friends to show off my work.

After the barbecue, I did not use the gazebo for several months. I was just plain tired of being out there.

The good news comes from all of the things I learned about construction, my own talents, the use of experts, and the cost of trial-and-error learning. The gazebo remains standing to this day.

## Measure Your Progress

Always know where you are on your journey. Do not just measure your project status but also your own degree of passion and commitment to your goal.

### Story: The Painter

A house painter came home after a rather difficult day at work. He was tired and not looking forward to returning to his job the following day. During dinner, his wife mentioned to him, for about the tenth time, the need for his own home to be painted. Although he was tired and simply wanted to relax in front of the television, he reluctantly agreed to spend time selecting the colors with her.

Two weeks later, his wife asked about the start date of the house painting, a question that she had asked numerous times since the selection of the colors. He pulled out his calendar and gave her a specific start date.

Fourteen days prior to the start date, she purchased the paint to have on hand when her husband jump-started the job. When the big day arrived, her husband seemed none too happy about beginning. After a brief pep talk, the painter went out and started on the front of the house. He worked for two days, completing the entire paint job on the front of the house. It looked beautiful, making his wife very happy.

The rest of the house remained unpainted for over six months. Everyone raved about the appearance of the front of the house, unaware that the other three sides remained untouched. In frustration, his wife contacted a professional painting contractor to finish the job. While the husband was on a two-day fishing trip with his friends, the remainder of the house was painted and the rival painter paid by his wife.

When he returned, she asked her husband to take out the trash, knowing he would go out back to reach the garbage cans. She was sure he would immediately notice that the painting job had been completed.

We can only imagine how the conversation went from this point forward. No doubt some marriage counseling was in their future.

Look at this example to spot the issues and the warning signals. Was the husband passionately committed to the goal? Did his actions suggest a high level of motivation? Did he create a timeline for the work? Did he believe that painting his own home was important?

Now consider how the painter's wife could have more effectively influenced her husband to get a swifter and more satisfactory outcome.

## Influence

Influence is the successful achievement of your desired outcome without alienating the person or persons you are trying to influence.

### Story: The Influencer

No one will be happy about being told, ordered, bribed, or harassed into having to take a specific action. You are all free spirits who prize your right to make your own choices. When you are coerced or unduly pressured by the needs of another person, without believing that it is also in your self-interest, you push back. Whether the issue is right or wrong matters less than the approach taken by the other person.

When my son was about nine years old, he asked me what I did for a living. My job title was sales executive for the largest and best insurance company in the United States. Knowing that my son would probably not understand either my title or daily responsibilities, I told him I got paid handsomely for spending each day influencing people.

He looked at me with an expression of total bewilderment. I could see I needed to *influence* his understanding.

"Remember the other night when you wanted to go to the movies and I said no?" He nodded. "Did you ask me again?" Once again a head nod gave his answer. "Then you told me that the movie was about a baseball player called Babe Ruth." He nodded again. "You told me your coach and the entire team were going to the movie and to a team pizza event and that you wanted to go to support the team." I told him, "You influenced me to change my mind, and we both went to the movie and the pizza party."

"I get it, Dad!" he said. He turned and started to walk away.

"Hey, where are you going?" I asked.

With a broad smile, he responded, "I am going to influence Mom into making some chocolate chip cookies."

Influencing is what each of us do all day every day. You do not achieve what you want without the skillful use of influence to achieve your primary goal while not offending the goals or feelings of others. It is not arguing, debating, or any of the other manipulative methods you may have used in the past. Influence is about creating a win-win outcome agreeable to everyone. Dale Carnegie brilliantly taught his students about the value of giving others what they want so that they, in turn, will provide you with what you want.

## Celebration

This is the needed enjoyment of your accomplishment. Create a *pause for applause* to reflect on your success. Enjoy every opportunity to feel good about yourself.

Have you ever seen anyone do a *happy dance*? This is the exuberant expression of achievement that sends a message to you, others, and the universe that you have done something of merit that has given you a supercharged moment of joy. It can be seen when you jump up as your son or daughter rounds the bases after hitting a home run or in a fist pump after a hard-fought victory or simply in a beaming smile after finishing a dreaded piano recital.

*Story: Ta-Da*

My oldest grandson, Jacoby, has taught me a great deal, one of the most important things being the celebration of little things. He is very physically gifted and fearless about trying new levels of achievement. At about three years old, he climbed rather high into a tree, steadied himself, threw his hands into the air, and loudly proclaimed a big, "*Ta-da!*" He was recognized for his skill, which established a consistent expression for the joyful success of each little thing.

## Recommendation

Start your own personal *ta-da* tradition. Each time you accomplish something, take a moment, throw your hands in the air, and proudly proclaim, "*Ta-da.*" Encourage others to do the same. When you hear a *ta-da*, stop what you are doing and give the proclaiming person congratulations, praise, and recognition on his or her new accomplishment. Both the performer and you will feel great.

Finally, take a few moments to strategically look at your success. Ask the important questions:

- What would I do again?
- What would I not repeat?
- What could I do better?
- Was the result worth the effort?
- How can I develop more efficiency?

Remember that everything starts with a thought that in turn creates a feeling. Feelings can be either good or bad. A good feeling brings joy, excitement, enthusiasm, commitment, and action. A bad feeling creates fear, trepidations, lack of confidence, and hesitation. You will experience both feelings on a daily basis. You get the opportunity to choose your thoughts, so choose wisely.

## The F-Word

*Fundamental: the elements that define belief*

A fundamental reality is that you must share this planet with about seven billion other people who have very differing opinions on life and how to live it. You cannot—and should never try to—change others to conform to your point of view. The best you can hope for is a level of tolerance that brings peace and value to each individual.

These same fundamentals serve as the guidelines for living. Regardless of all other factors, all creatures that inhabit this earth must obey the natural laws of the universe. There is no choice. One of those laws of nature is that you will receive what you give. Love given is love received.

You may not understand the actions of others, but you must understand that they have been given the same right as you, to freely determine who and what they want to be.

Confidence in yourself and your ability to occasionally reinvent yourself to any changing situation will assure you that you will adapt as needed to prosper in life.

## Timeless Wisdom

*Create a pause for applause.*
When you accomplish your goal, take just a little time to celebrate your accomplishment.

Office practice: Purchase a trophy that reads "Team Member of the Day." On day one, award the trophy, in the presence of the other team members, for something a team member did really well. On the second day, it is the responsibility of the trophy holder to spot another team member doing something well and give him or her the trophy as a symbol of recognition. Repeat daily.

People love to be acknowledged, thanked, appreciated, and recognized.

*What you think about, you become.*
Remember the expression, "Be careful what you wish for; you just might get it." The real wisdom behind this saying is that whatever you focus on, you will draw to you.

Thoughts are powerful. Repeated thinking on the same thought commands it into reality. So if you constantly love, you will receive love. If you are constantly finding worries, the universe will constantly give you cause for worry.

# FOUND TREASURE

*Be very selective about your thoughts and the input you allow to enter your mind.*

---

*People will not remember what you said but they will remember how you said it and how it made them feel.*

*—Maya Angelou*

---

This has got to be one of the most important pieces of advice in this entire book. Your words and actions invoke strong feelings in others. Those feelings will be predicated on how you delivered the message. What did you intend? Was it said with sincerity and in a calm manner? Did it create a better understanding, or did it create pushback or anger?

This is truly a matter of style as well as execution. The message will be lost if it is delivered in an overly angry or aggressive manner. It will also become suspect if the message is insensitive or self-serving.

Make others feel great! Be very intentional with your words and actions.

# Effective Decision Making

It is acutely important that you not make decisions rashly in the heat of the moment, driven by agitated emotions, devoid of thoughtful attention to the potential positive or negative consequences.

---

*If decision making is flawed and dysfunctional, decisions will go awry.*

*—Carly Fiorina*

---

## Where to Make Decisions

People may approach you after a meeting, at a social engagement, or even while on a family outing to get an answer to a question or to voice a concern. They catch you when you are distracted. Do not make any quick or hasty decisions under these circumstances.

Identify a very specific location where you make all your decisions. It can be at your desk at work or maybe in your home office.

These situations can also cause you to become flustered or embarrassed, leading to a poorly thought out, hasty, and erroneous answer.

FOUND TREASURE

*Story: The Surprise Date*

As a junior in high school, a female classmate stopped me while we were walking to class one day. She was a very nice girl who caught me off guard by asking me to go to the Sadie Hawkins dance with her in two weeks. I did not want to embarrass her or myself in front of my friend, so I sputtered through a response.

As we were walking away, my friend said he wanted to see the look on my girlfriend's face when I told her I had awkwardly accepted a dance date with another girl. When I challenged him, I suddenly realized that in my nervous response I had told this nice classmate I would accept her offer.

I sought some counseling from my older sister, who took great joy in seeing me in a bad situation. I rehearsed a speech for two days to unravel my acceptance. I made my call and rushed through my acceptance reversal. I felt terrible because I knew it had taken all the courage she could muster to ask me in the first place.

I felt so lousy that I did not go to the dance at all, much to the unhappiness of my actual girlfriend.

## Listen to Your Gut

Your instincts were given to you by God to warn you about impending danger. When you feel uncomfortable about a decision you need to make, pull back to give it more consideration. The universe is constantly sending you caution signals that should never be ignored.

*Story: The Night Ninja*

A young man was put in charge of a high school social function that had a limited budget. He wanted the event to be a big success so he decided that a gazebo should be built in the middle of the dance floor to create charm and to house the king and queen of the dance.

With a meager budget, the decision was made to go to a new construction site after dark to borrow some needed lumber. The ninja theft went as planned. The wood was stored in a hidden spot. Luckily, the young man had a conscience, which kept him up several nights in a row. He wisely decided to correct his mistake by returning the lumber to its original source. To his good fortune, he didn't experience any criminal consequences for his poor decision.

*What feels wrong is wrong!* These feelings come from your soul. Doing the right thing, at the right time, and for the right reason is generally defensible.

---

*Inability to make decisions is one of the principal reasons executives fail. Deficiency in decision- making rank higher than lack of specific knowledge or technical know-how as an indicator of leadership failure.*

–John C. Maxwell

---

## When in Doubt, Seek Counsel

Sometimes you are just too involved in a situation to remain objective. You may also discover that your lack of experience renders you incapable of moving forward. This is the time to seek a reliable third party who is both detached from the situation and who has some life experience that might be beneficial.

Select your advisors wisely. Use a person you trust who has no vested interest in the outcome of the situation. Select someone who can really be trusted to keep your conversation confidential.

### Story: Nervous Nancy

Nancy told her very best girlfriend that she was nervous going out on a date with an older, more experienced man. Her best friend's boyfriend was a close pal of Nancy's intended date. All of the information Nancy shared with her girlfriend was then passed on to her boyfriend and eventually to his pal. When these shared conversations were accidentally, and embarrassingly, revealed the evening of the date, everybody was angry. The evening was spoiled.

## Review Decisions with Superiors when Ethical Issues Are Involved

Some decisions may come with a potential conflict of interest. Whenever your decision will have an influence on you personally or professionally, share the decision with your superior before making your final decision or taking action. Tell your superior what you intend to do and ask if he or she can support your decision.

This removes any suspicion that you acted in your own self-interest rather than in the interest of the other parties involved.

Make note of the actual conversation and the support you received from your superior. This will be helpful if your personal interests are questioned at a later time. (If you cannot express your solution with your superior, it is more than likely that your decision is self-serving and potentially inappropriate.)

## Visit with the Impacted Parties Before Going Public with Your Decision

Anyone impacted by one of your decisions has the right to hear the decision from you before it is made public. This conversation should take place in person and in private. Never catch anyone by surprise, especially in public.

*Pause, ponder, consult, think through it well, understand the consequence, know the benefit, and take a second look at it again for it takes a little mistake to cause a deep regret.*
                                                        *—Ernest Agyemang Yeboah*

## Check in with the Impacted Parties

After the decision has been made and communicated, check back with the impacted parties. See if they need any further clarity or need to ask any questions. Every decision is easier to accept when the people impacted truly believe they are respected.

## Not Making a Decision Can Become a Nightmare

The longer a decision goes unanswered, the greater the pain it will cause. Some people think that not making a decision is all right. On the contrary, making no decision is making a decision of procrastination.

*Not making a decision means forgoing an opportunity.*
                                                        *—Aulig Ice*

Problems rarely go away on their own. Quite to the contrary, often they intensify. Treat making a needed decision like a top priority to avoid confusing the message behind the decision or sending the wrong message to the intended party.

Time delays may suggest a lack of attention to another's concern. It may also be perceived as a silent acceptance of the action in question.

# It Takes Courage to Be a Decision Maker

For most people, it is a very good day when they have to make a limited number of decisions. Decision making is difficult. When each decision is made, it will potentially impact a great number of people. No one wants to be considered the bad guy in the decision-making process.

Many people delay or ignore making a decision. That indecision is a decision to not face the situation at hand. This is an all too common way to avoid confrontational conversations, unwanted emotional outbursts, and rejection.

It is very important that the proper amount of research be done prior to any decision. Make sure all aspects of the situation and any necessary subsequent decision are considered before moving forward.

# Leaders Must Make Decisions in the Moment

*If you care about what people think about you, you will end up being their slave. Reject and pull your own rope.*

—Aulig Ice

Unfortunately, life periodically surprises you with an experience you do not anticipate or desire. The true test of a leader is having the confidence to select the prudent and needed course of action. He or she must ask for and receive the support of his or her followers. This is an awesome responsibility.

True leaders do not shrink away from decisions, but they also have enough wisdom not to inflame a volatile situation.

# What Was I Thinking?

*Split-second decision making sets winners apart from losers.*
—Stephen Richards, *Six-Figure Success: Time to Think Big—You Can Do It*

How many times have you allowed your decisions to be made by an emotional impulse in the heat of the moment and lived to regret it? In a split second, your life can be permanently altered by an irrational decision that leads to disaster.

## Story: Party Time

Betty accepted a date with Tom because she thought he was cute. She did not know much about him except that he was very often absent from school and wasn't involved with any of the typical activities that Betty enjoyed. He was a loner and appeared to be somewhat of a rebel.

Betty thought it was time for her to shake her good girl image by hanging out with someone who would have everyone talking.

Tom picked Betty up for their date, arriving nearly a half hour late. He was dressed in old and dirty jeans, a plain white T-shirt, and a raggedy old ball cap, which was turned around with the bill in the back.

Tom would not tell Betty where they were going. He simply told her that they were meeting up with a few of his friends to party. They drove way outside of town to a regional park that Betty had never seen before, where they met about a dozen people.

Tom jumped out of his car and was immediately greeted by several of his friends. Betty trailed behind. Tom did not even bother introducing Betty to any of his friends. She felt uncomfortable and out of place. Tom was gone for about ten minutes before returning to Betty. He let her know that he had needed to handle a little business before he was ready to give her all of his attention. From his jacket, he produced a small plastic bag filled with what appeared to be pills. He told her she should take one as he popped two into his own mouth.

Betty had never used drugs in her entire life. She felt the eyes of everyone at the party staring at her to see if she would take the drug, making her an accepted member of the group. Tom then pulled a pint bottle of whiskey from his back pocket to use to wash the pill down.

What do you think Betty did? What were the warnings signs to Betty that this evening was going in the wrong direction? What were her possible options, and what were the potential consequences of her decision?

## Story: Desperate Cheater

Sue was a senior at the local university, where she was studying to get her bachelor of science degree so she could take her LSAT exam to get into a prestigious law school. She wanted to be a corporate attorney like her father.

Sue was really struggling in her advanced physics class. She had been watching her normal B+ grade drop with each exam. She just could not seem to capture the material. Her marginally passing grade was contingent upon receiving a high grade on the final exam. She was desperate. If she actually failed the class, she would not graduate.

She would also not be able to start the legal internship that had been arranged by her father.

Knowing she was in a very tight spot, a friend put her in contact with another student who could secure an advanced copy of the final exam for a reasonable cost. When Sue tried to get details, she was met with silence. The offer was made again, for $500. Panic set in. With what seemed to be no other option, Sue finally agreed to the arrangement.

Unfortunately, Sue had not been talking to a fellow student. She had unknowingly been arranging her crime with an undercover member of campus security.

Sue was reported to the chancellor's office. She was expelled from the university and not given her semester credits for work completed. She was ordered off the campus within twenty-four hours.

What do you think happened to Sue's plans of a law degree?

*The Keys to Making Sound Decisions*

- Do not act hastily.
- Never act before finding out all the facts.
- Let logic trump emotion.
- Define who will win or lose as a result of your decision.
- Determine if your decision is self-serving.
- Decide whether you can live with the consequences.
- Are you willing to make your decision widely known?
- Can you support your decision with a truthful motive?

# The F-Word

*Framework: the processes we design that define our standards*

In order to make viable, clear, and acceptable decisions, a leader must rely on well-defined standards that are relevant to the circumstances.

Without personal standards, there is absolutely no basis upon which to make a decision.

Monday morning quarterbacking will surely follow each decision you make. In the calm reflection of a situation, devoid of real-time emotional entanglements, the actions taken may come under question. Other possible options may be revealed and preferred. This process cannot freeze you from making a needed decision. Neither should such a decision lack support from your superiors because of new options devised after the fact.

Decisions are made in the moment, heavily influenced by the emotions at the time. At this critical instant, you must go with the feelings that come from your soul.

---

*Avoid making a decision when you are either mad or sad.*

*—Anonymous*

---

When questioned about motive after the fact, it is very important that the decision maker can justify his or her behavior without a conflict of self-interest. If the decision maker acted on the information at the time, considering the impact on others rather than personal self-interests, the decision or conclusion will normally meet the standard of acceptance or tolerance.

Decisions made for the personal benefit of the decision maker will always be suspect.

## Timeless Wisdom

*Fear is created by what-if and why questions.*

What-if and why questions rarely have good answers. If they have any answer, it will generally lead to more and similar questions.

What-if questions allow you to dream up the most unlikely and terrible possibilities.

Why questions seek the motive behind an action. If the reason does not support your vision of life, you will not accept the why answer.

You have better things to do with your life. Accept what you must accept and move on.

*Motive linked to behavior clarifies intent*

All good crime programs seek the criminal's motive. This is the big why question. If you can identify motive, you can see the true reason for someone's behavior.

When you act, does your real motive support a personal benefit or the benefit of others? Was your motive one of love or fear? Why do you do what you do?

Motive is the secret to understanding behavior.

*Poor judgment or lack of attention to details destroys trust.*

Poor judgment is the cause of every negative thing that has ever happened in your life.

You are a decision-making machine. You are compelled to constantly make decisions. You simply cannot stop making decisions for fear of being wrong.

To avoid labeling your children or others as either bad or good, use this method. After a child or person takes a specific action, ask him or her whether he or she made a good choice or a bad choice. This labels the *choice,* not the child or the person, as bad or good. It also gives you the opportunity to reinforce the need for thought before the child or person acts, which will help him or her avoid negative consequences.

Good judgment after a poor judgment is called learning.

# Having Difficult Conversations

It is very natural for people to avoid any conversation that they have predetermined will be uncomfortable or confrontational. You have been taught by your youthful training to be polite and sensitive to the feelings of others. This training has pushed you to conversational habits that have made the complicated art of conversing more difficult. You likely use a multitude of social maneuvers, which often muddles the message; creating more confusion than if nothing had been said at all.

There are several important points to consider when having any conversation. The words spoken during a conversation only convey a small portion of the message that the speaker wishes to send. Choose your words and delivery wisely.

The following are some of the common methods used by many people that might be described as conversations. Read them to see if any are common practices you use.

## Words Are Powerful

Here are several words and verbal methods to avoid:

- Raising your voice is forceful and aggressive and conveys anger and frustration. It will serve as a trigger for more aggressive behavior by the listener.

- Using foul language is never acceptable in any civil conversation. It suggests an inability of the speaker to articulate his or her thoughts.
- Talking too much. It is better to ask questions to draw out the important elements of the conversation rather than dominating the conversation. Some people talk too much so they do not have to hear unwanted comments of others.
- Personalizing the conversation or talking about how the listener's actions impact only you. Conversations that are "I" driven convey a self-centered motive. Seek to measure the emotional reactions of all the parties involved in the conversation. Ask, do not assume.
- Personal attacks on a person's beliefs, appearance, religion, ethnicity, etc., are surefire ways to bring a conversation to an immediate and very emotional halt. Suspend your judgment and speak your observations. Judgment creates enemies, not collaborators.
- Using angry words such as *hate, stupid, moronic*, etc. Emotional damage is the most effective way to repress meaningful exchange. These words are designed to hurt or shock.
- Being vague and long-winded. People have a limited attention span to absorb the important thoughts of the conversation. Long talks cause people to zone out and lose interest. Say what you have to say in the simplest and shortest method possible.
- Avoid common guilt words such as *should* and *have to*. They strongly imply judgment on the part of the speaker. The other conversational partner will feel that he or she is being talked down to, like a child in trouble.

## Location

The location of the conversation will heavily influence its emotional impact. Here are a few tips for selecting the right location for the conversation:

- Select a neutral and mutually agreed upon location. If the conversation could turn angry, make sure you meet your conversational partner in a public setting where common courtesy will repress emotional outbursts.
- Always praise in public. Recognizing good behavior or performance is a great way to build confidence.

- Criticize in private. Criticism, even if warranted, is difficult to accept when other people are around. When criticizing, be very mindful of your environment.
- Select a public environment if the conversation could result in intense emotions. A public environment is important to avoid the negative effect of you said, she said. It is also a good method to avoid potential physical threat.
- Have a third party present to verify the contents and reaction of the conversation, especially if you fear the conversation could lead to physical hostility or future litigation.

## Body Language

Body language is another major element of the message. Here are several types of body language to avoid:

- Lack of eye contact implies a person is either timid about the conversation or is not telling the truth. (Direct eye contact gives credibility to your words.)
- Crossed arms suggest a blocked mind, irritation, or resistance. It also may suggest defiance.
- When your eyes roam and focus on passersby, you are being distracted by activities and not part of the conversation, which makes it seem like you do not want to be there or are bored or disinterested.
- Glancing at your smart phone or taking a call minimizes the importance of the conversation
- Leaning into the conversation suggests that the listener is more eager to respond than to continue to listen. This can suggest the speaker is dominating the conversation.
- Rolling of the eyes to demonstrate disapproval signals disagreement and judgment
- Hand gestures distract from the words spoken
- Talking under your breathe may suggest distain for the speaker or the conversation
- Sighing is an obvious signal that the listener has disconnected from the conversation

# Types of Conversations

People always use their personal value systems when they determine whether something is right or wrong. Often their values will not align with the values of others. This immediately creates a highly intense and contentious environment. That is why most experts tell you to avoid conversations about religion or politics.

## Story: The Judgmental Wife

A close personal friend had a very serious automobile accident. He was hospitalized and spent a prolonged period of time in the intensive care unit. Only immediate family members could visit him during that time.

As the victim's best friend, you did not come to the hospital after you returned from a business trip about a week after the accident. When the victim was moved out of intensive care, you immediately came to the hospital to visit your injured buddy.

As you entered the hospital room, the spouse of the victim immediately confronted you saying, "Well, Tom, it's about time! Your best friend is seriously injured but you didn't come to the hospital. I'm not sure that he wants to see you."

Passing judgment on another person is a very bad habit. Making assumptions and representing the judgment of another person often fails to project the true sentiment of the unspoken third party.

## Too Personal Too Soon Conversation

Have you ever experienced a conversation that brought intimate information into a conversation without your encouragement or any pretext?

For example, picture yourself casually sitting at the counter of your local diner, reading the newspaper while enjoying a morning coffee when a young woman in her thirties comes in and takes the seat next to you. You exchange smiles. Her attention goes immediately to the menu to make her early morning selection. You continue to read the news.

"It's a crazy world," she says, glancing at the headlines on your paper.

"Pardon me?" you respond, not clear about whether she is talking to you, asking you a question, or making a statement.

"Look at all that terrible news today. Murders, a country in bankruptcy, dirty politicians—the world is a mess!"

You really do not want to do anything but read your paper, but to be polite, you nod and say: "Yeah, things are a little rough."

"A little rough," she says. "They should write a story about my life. Then people would know what a really rough life is like. I haven't been working for the last six months, so I have been sleeping on a friend's couch at night and scanning the want ads during the day. I can't find anything!"

"I am sorry to hear that. Can I buy you a cup of coffee?" you say, motioning the waitress over while pointing to her coffee cup.

"Thanks" she says. "I am sorry to be a Debbie Downer, but things are lousy for me right now. I broke up with my boyfriend a month ago after being together for four years. I caught him cheating on me with some gal that tends bar where he works. I dumped his ass. Now he won't stop calling me to try to get back together. I don't want anything to do with him. Would you take back a girlfriend after she cheated on you?"

## Talking to Yourself

Around the office you have an administrative person who is constantly talking, whether there is someone at her desk or not. She talks very low, almost in a whisper, pretty much all of the time.

She expects you to be listening whenever you are in close proximity to her cubicle even though the comments do not appear to be directed at you. You find yourself continually asking her to repeat herself because you do not understand what she is saying. She then tells you either that she was not talking to you or that you need to pay more attention. It is really uncomfortable to find yourself in either conversation.

You find yourself avoiding any reason to be near her cubicle in an effort to prevent any conversation at all.

## The Me-Want Conversation

You have always had an open door policy at your office. You understand the importance of people having access to you. You want to let them know you care about them. Unfortunately, this creates a lot of interruptions during the day that force you to stay late each night to finish your work.

One particular person comes by your office two or three times a day. The pattern is always the same.

"Hey, could I have just a minute of your time?" says your visitor.

"Sure, what can I do for you?" you say.

Without any small talk or personal inquiry about how your day is going, the visitor will ask you to give information or your opinion on a topic of concern.

You normally have what they need, which you volunteer willingly. As soon as your associate gets an answer, she turns and departs.

One particular day, you block the door so that your visitor cannot leave your office.

The visitor is surprised when you say, "You come in to my office multiple times a day asking for either input or advice on an issue of importance to you. I don't mind being your mentor or *thinking partner*, but you never ask if there's anything I need. You come across as self-centered and insensitive."

"Oh my goodness!" responds the visitor.

"I know you're a good person and that you truly care about people, but your obsession with getting your agenda item handled without checking with a person about his or her professional or personal needs gives the impression that you are cold and self-serving," you say.

"So people see me as cold and selfish?" the visitor gasps. "That isn't my intent!"

You pause and then say, "That's why I am bringing it to your attention. I realize it's simply part of your business methodology, but just a little small talk or interest in the agenda of the other person will normally pay you some tremendous dividends. I have taken the risk of being honest with you because I truly care about you. I know your intentions are very different than perceived."

"I appreciate your honesty," the visitor says as tears well up in her eyes.

"The good news is you can easily change your behavior to make your approach friendlier and mutually beneficial. Slow down a little. Give people a little time. Just make sure you ask how you can help them."

The visitor thanks you with a big hug and departs from your office. To her credit, she takes the comments in a positive manner. She modifies her approach to the point where everyone in the entire office notices the change.

## The Complainer Conversation

"Did you see the way the boss has Smitty following him like a lapdog? Smitty is the biggest kiss up in the office. He never does his work and is always getting special favors from the boss. I don't get it! Is everyone blind to his manipulation?"

## The Trap Conversation

This is a conversation created around vague questions that are not clearly understood until you are already committed.

"Hey, Harry, are you a baseball fan?" says Tom.

Harry says, "Yeah, Giants."

"Do you go to many games, Harry?" asks Tom.

"Whenever I can," replies Harry.

Tom stares at Harry and says, "I know you have season tickets, so I am happy to use them whenever you can't go, like Friday when you will be out of town. Can I have them for Friday's game?"

## The Insecure Conversation

This is a conversation in which the person you are visiting with continues to probe for compliments to make his- or herself feel better. The persons asks you numerous questions that are intended to draw out how you view him or her.

"I didn't think I did very well giving the presentation today. How do you think I did? Did the crowd seem to get my key points?"

The classic conversation that gets a lot of attention in this category is, "Do you think this dress makes my butt look big?" You should get clarity before you respond: "Do you want your butt to look bigger?" The answer to your question will determine your response and your honesty.

## A Forced Conversation

Many people are very sheltered and do not want to have their personal feelings exposed. This may not meet the expectations of another, so they force a conversation, often described as the where-do-I-stand conversation.

This kind of conversation can often bring an end to a relationship. The reluctant person will be angered for being pressured or bullied and not respected by his or her conversation partner's behavior.

"I think I have been a loyal employee and a real asset to the company over the last year. You have not mentioned any bonus or promotion for next year. I would really like to know where I stand so I can plan my future."

These conversations force a response. In many cases the silence of the reluctant participant is the answer.

### The Or-Else Conversation

This is a conversation that tends to lead to an unwanted consequence if there is no agreement with the speaker's position.

"We have been working together for five years. I have always had your back and even worked for you when you had some personal issues that you had to handle. So I think you owe me some additional help to complete my reports by the end of the day," said Joyce to her coworker Donna.

"Joyce, I would help you, but I have reports of my own that need to be done by the end of the day. I'm sorry I can't help, but I would be happy to help you next time," said Donna.

Joyce's emotions flared. "Fine, Donna! Don't expect my help in the future."

### It's All About Me Conversation

Bill and Sam were having a conversation during a break at their monthly company meeting. Bill congratulated Sam on the special award he had been given earlier in the day for his high sales performance.

"Thanks, Bill," said Sam. "It really was poorly done. I set a new record for sales, so they have me stand in the meeting and then give me an inexpensive certificate to commemorate my accomplishment. That is not the way the top sales performer should be treated."

### The One-Up Conversation

Suzanne was joyfully telling a group of her friends about the hole in one she got playing golf on her last vacation. This was her first hole in one, which made her feel really great about her accomplishment.

Her friends responded with high fives and supportive comments. Ann, one of the better golfers in the group, spoke up to let the group know that she had four holes in one, so she knew how exciting the first one was for Suzanne.

## The Critics Review Conversation

You tell Pam how you are so excited about being asked to the junior prom by Matt Sanchez. "He asked me just after history class. He was very nervous and could hardly get the words out."

Pam, who has not been asked to the prom, begins to criticize the silly and unimportant junior prom, followed by several demeaning comments about Matt. You are astounded. You know Pam would love to go to the prom and just two weeks ago she confessed to having a major crush on Matt.

You see, people disguise their personal disappointments by belittling an event or person. They are embarrassed by their predicament, so they try to minimize the good fortune of others.

## The Phony Conversation

This is when one person tells another to take the lead in the conversation and then follows with an attempt to change his or her mind.

Mike came home and saw that his wife, Barbara, had had a difficult day handling the kids. He volunteered to take her to dinner. She was thrilled.

"Where would you like to go to eat?" Mike said.

"I don't care," Barbara responded. "I want you to decide."

Mike says, "Okay, we'll go to that little Italian place in the mall."

"Oh, Mike, I don't really want Italian food," said Barbara.

"How about Mexican food?" Mike said.

Barbara sighed.

"Okay, Barbara, where do you want to go?"

Barbara responded by saying, "It doesn't matter to me. I am just glad we are going out together."

In Mike's attempt to get valuable input from Barbara, he unwittingly entered the dangerous *no-win zone*. Lurking behind this conversation could be a series of issues that will not lead to a fair, quick, or satisfactory decision.

*Warning:* Next time, Mike should rephrase his question into a statement, "Barbara, you have had a very hard day, so I would like to take you to dinner at the Italian place at the mall. I'll call right now to make a reservation."

## There Is Only One Answer Conversation

"Do you want to go to the opera next Friday?" John says.

John knows I really hate opera, thinks Trudy. "I really would prefer to just go to the movies," she says.

John frowns and says, " Well, I think we have a problem. I already purchased the opera tickets."

There was no reason for John to even ask Trudy for her opinion because he had already decided what was going to happen. Trudy suddenly feels trapped and thinks John manipulated her to get his own way.

*Warning:* This is a very common practice. The person who asks the question normally wants a positive response. If he or she receives something other than the anticipated answer, he or she will begin to use emotions to change it.

The person who receives the question knows what will happen if he or she does not respond as expected.

This repeated behavior will generally lead to a major breakdown in communication. The person asking the questions will be seen as pushing his or her own agenda, while the person getting questioned will be reluctant to even listen to the question.

Everyone really wants to be able to answer a question honestly. We also want our answers to be accepted rather than judged as incorrect.

Everyone needs to thoroughly understand that if you ask a question, you must accept the answer even if you dislike it. If the answer is not accepted, you will see the person begin to avoid a conversation by answering, "Whatever," or getting argumentative. If this kind of behavior persists, it will not be long before all honest communication in the relationship comes to a screeching halt.

## The Giving Advice Conversation

People may come to you for advice because they respect you and value your life experience. They put you in a challenging position. No person comes to you for advice without a preconceived outcome in mind. You must ascertain whether that person wants to have you decide for him or her or validate the decision he or she has already made, or truly wants your opinion.

*Warning*: All three of these options are dangerous for the advice giver. Be cautious deciding something for anyone other than yourself. If you are right, the person will take the credit for the decision. If you are wrong, the person will blame you. Avoid this dilemma.

*The Termination Conversation*

Before entering into a potential or assumed termination conversation, refer to the human resource department experts available to you, state employment law, or consult an attorney. The information provided below is generalized and has not been written with specific legal scrutiny. Always protect yourself before taking action.

It is never easy to be the sender of bad news. Most of us will procrastinate or avoid such a conversation, hoping the issues will some how disappear.

This conversation is generally as hard for the sender as it is on the receiver. A sleepless night often accompanies such a task.

When terminating the employment of a person, consider these important insights:

- You don't terminate someone; he or she terminates him- or herself. The person's behaviors, skills, actions, or inactions have sealed his or her fate. You are only announcing the obvious.
- Valued personnel are rarely terminated unless the business itself is in real jeopardy. A lack of passion, dedication, and positive results of the employee have led to this outcome. Had this employee given you more value, his or her termination would be unnecessary.
- Termination normally follows numerous and repeated warnings. Termination rarely comes as a surprise to the employee.
- Don't use false flattery to soften the message. Stop telling someone how much you appreciate him or her, followed by the delivery of a pink slip. It is insincere and insulting.
- If poor job performance is the cause of termination, do not tell the terminated employee that you will recommend him or her to others. This shows a major lack of personal integrity on your part. Hypocrisy creates added tension, often leading to hostility.

Here is a sample termination conversation:

"June, as you know, we have had several conversations about your work quality, office demeanor, and tardiness over the last several weeks. So I want to ask you a very direct question. Are you really happy working here?"

Allow the employee to respond. If you see a sincere response that leads you to reconsider, say, "What can you do then to resolve the issues we have discussed so many times?" Again, allow the employee to respond.

Prevent the reopening of old wounds. Do not start or allow the *blame game* to take over the conversation. Insist that the employee be specific about any corrective action he or she will use to resolve the issues of concern. Establish a probationary period with a specific beginning and end. See the tips on the next page.

If the conversation seems to conclude with the need to separate, say, "I think we have agreed that your current employment is not a good fit for you or the business. I'll give you the opportunity to resign if you chose."

If the employee fails to resign, let him or her know that you will terminate his or her employment effective as of a certain date!

Throughout the conversation, follow these important tips:

- Never use attitude exclusively as grounds for termination. It is subjective and open to excuse making and interpretation.
- Remain calm and speak softly.
- Have the conversation in private.
- Do not discuss specific incidents that have been identified in the past. This is not the time for detail or debate.
- Keep an ear out for an insubordinate tone. Insubordination in a termination conversation can show the defensive nature of the employee and also a lack of respect for you.
- If reconsideration is given, clearly outline the specific changes and deadlines the employee must achieve to continue his or her employment. Construct a mutually agreeable action plan and timeline. Be specific on what will be measured and how it will be tracked. Have the employee sign and date both a copy for you and another for him or her. Set a specific appointment date to review the employee's corrective action.
- If you decide to terminate the employee or the employee decides to quit, agree to the proper amount of severance pay, supervise the immediate collection of his or her belongings, take back all business equipment, reclaim the security cards and keys, and see the employee to the door. Lock the door behind him or her if the encounter was hostile.

- If the employee is terminated, do not have them continue to come to work. By allowing his or her presence in the office, you risk breaches in security that may harm your business.
- Inform your other company employees that the terminated employee has moved on and will no longer be associated with the business.
- Do not share the reasons for termination with other team members or customers.
- Remove passwords and access codes to your computer site.
- Have the office locks changed.
- Alter security codes on business alarm systems.
- Send notification to anyone else (vendors or clients) simply announcing that the employee is no longer associated with your business.
- Do not share any details about the employee's departure with anyone. If asked simply say, "John decided to look at some other career opportunities."
- Do not bad mouth the former employee to anyone.
- If contacted by potential employers wanting to hire your former employee, do not share any details. Identify the time period that the former employee worked for you. If you are asked whether you would rehire this person, answer with either a yes or a no.
- Document your personnel file with all relevant dates, interactions, and notes of events and conversations that occurred. Do not comment on personalities, personal traits, or flaws. Be professional and specific. Do not editorialize or give unnecessary information.
- Retain the file for your own protection in the future.
- Move on. Do not dwell on the incident. Find a suitable replacement and create a fresh start for you and your retained employees.
- Always keep a hot list of potential employees.
- Determine what needs to be done differently in the future.

## The On-the-Same-Page Conversation

When someone says to you that you and he are not on the same page, realize what he is really saying is that you are not on his page. Bring that to his attention.

Realize that you are in need of mutually defined end result. How you will achieve the goal will be a subject of lively debate. Agree that the result is more important than the egos of the debaters.

Agree to give each person ample uninterrupted time to express how he or she believes the goal can be accomplished.

Set ground rules of mutual respect.

Agree not to personalize the discussion. Remain focused on the goal.

*Do not try to win.* For you to win, someone else has to lose. Approach everything in a win-win method.

Listen with an unbiased attitude. Do not judge. Instead, spend your listening time observing. Then review your outline of needed action with an uninvolved third party for advice, input, and impartiality.

Setting the ground rules prior to the conversation will bring about positive results. It will also aid in fostering an attitude of cooperation and collaboration.

## The I'm Sorry Conversation

"I am sorry, but I just wanted to be liked by my friends." How many times have you heard this halfhearted kind of apology from your teenagers? An apology should not be laced with excuses or rationalizations. The word *but* renders all of the words before it useless.

An apology states what was done, acknowledges the hurt one's actions have caused, and requests forgiveness.

It normally should be said with the fewest words possible and great humility and followed by silence. All apologies should be made in person, eye to eye. This demonstrates the sincerity of the apologizer. The person apologizing also receives the respect of the receiver, who knows how difficult it is to say you are sorry face-to-face.

*Warning:* During this conversation, refrain from bringing up the dirty deeds of the past. Do not try to counterbalance any of your wrongdoing with previous offenses by the person receiving the apology.

If you are wrong, take the reaction of the offended party in respectful silence. This will allow your relationship to heal in the shortest time possible.

## Influencing a Supervisor Conversation

"Mr. Smith, I really appreciate all of the time and effort you put into the presentation you gave to our group this afternoon. It had a wonderful and meaningful message. It actually sparked a few thoughts in me. Would you give me a minute to share my thoughts?"

Realize that most people put a great deal of time and effort into preparing a presentation. As they formulate their thoughts, they have convinced themselves that their thoughts and ideas are the best. When challenged, they may become aggressive or defensive, rude, and uninterested in what they perceive to be criticism.

To give input, you must take the following steps:

- Ask and receive permission.
- Avoid inflammatory comments when the issues are sensitive.
- Recognize it is easy to be a critic but often very difficult to be a problem solver.
- Measure your credibility to give input. Are you coming from a position of personal knowledge, experience, and success?
- Offer constructive ideas to enhance the plan rather than offering a completely different plan all together.
- Rather than being hungry for credit, strive for results.
- Offer your time and work to contribute to the plan or the input you have given.
- If you have time, research your suggested items for feasibility.
- Collaborate; do not dominate.
- Offer your criticism, comments, and input in a private environment. No one accepts criticism from the audience in a public setting.

Here are some key elements to a successful conversation:

- Keep in mind that people will forget the words that are said, but they will remember forever how those words made them feel.
- Stay calm. The person who remains calm and suppresses emotion will always appear to be the best and most effective communicator.
- Review the words spoken, location, and body language.
- Rehearse the conversation prior to the actual encounter.
- Be sensitive to the emotions of the listener, but do not let his or her emotions change the purpose or outcome of the conversation.

## The F-Word

*Friend: the community of man*
Conversations and storytelling are the most common ways you communicate with your fellow human beings. The words you speak are powerful and can express how you feel. Words can cause considerable harm if not managed properly.

It is very important to keep the following tips in mind:

- Know your audience.
- Avoid sarcasm! It's often funny for the sender but not for the receiver.
- Comments about people and their ideas cause immediate friction.
- Holding your tongue is often the best strategy.
- Don't tell people; ask them.
- Don't speak for someone else.
- Use terms, expressions, and stories to fit your audience.
- Lace your conversations with many descriptive words to captivate your audience.
- Use humor when you're good at it and when it is appropriate.
- Foul language is called "foul" for a reason.

Finally, remember this great piece of advice: You never have to say you're sorry for something you did not say.

## Timeless Wisdom

*Holding your tongue is a useful strategy.*
Silence is powerful. It is disarming for a person who is trying to intentionally pull you into a confrontation or dispute. Silence relieves you of having to apologize or do damage control after a conversation.

*Warning:* Do not remain silent with the other party, only to go to a third party to vent your venom. That third party might have a desire to share your thoughts with others.

*Enthusiasm conveys the conviction of truth.*

When you get excited, others join you. Your excitement, or what is often called *passion*, draws people to you. Your dedication to an idea or action inspires others to excel. Youthful enthusiasm can energize anything.

Find the excitement again! Do not simply do something because you have to; do it because you want to. Listen to your inner child to find the joy in every moment.

*Get excited!*

*Know your audience before you speak.*

Not knowing your audience makes it highly probable that your words will irritate or alienate some of your listeners. Speakers who fail to research the motivation of the listeners will be challenged to capture the interest and attention of the crowd.

A common mistake is the use of inappropriate attempts at humor. Your humorous material must be scrutinized to avoid slurs, vulgarity, etc.

The best speaker is the one who thoroughly knows his or her audience before drafting a speech. Do some research!

# The Five *F*'s for a Responsible Life

It is clear that the greatest teaching method in the world is the process of regular experimentation. You are here to fully experience life, not to simply observe it. To truly experience anything, you must make decisions that are followed by effort and action. Each decision will lead to a consequence. You hope your experiences bring you success, happiness, and personal benefits. You are also aware that you may encounter failure.

Both success and failure are great instructors in life. We duplicate our successes to have similar results and to climb to higher levels of performance. We use failure to recalibrate our behavior.

Let's examine a few obvious success stories to illustrate how current success is the greatest predictor of future success.

*Story: Mildred*

Mildred is a very productive team member of an engineering group at a moderately sized technology firm in Silicon Valley. Because of a lack of sales and rising material costs, the directors of the company announce the need to reduce personnel. Each employee will have to reinterview for his or her position. The goal of this process is a 25 percent reduction in personnel.

When Mildred goes to her interview, the interviewers realize the following things about her:

- She has received the highest evaluation scores of anyone in her team, ranking in the top 20 percent in the entire company
- Mildred has a very low absentee record
- She has been awarded two special bonuses for recommending operational changes that saved the company $150,000 annually
- She has been a loyal and trusted employee for the last seven years.
- She heads the annual Red Cross blood drive each year.
- She has an impressive continuing education plan that has kept her current on the most up-to-date technology software.

Mildred's interview takes only ten minutes even though each interview is allotted forty-five minutes. Because of her excellent performance, the interviewers had already predetermined that Mildred was a keeper. They even offer her a promotion.

It is clear that Mildred established herself as a valued employee. Her reputation and actual results played a large role in her continued employment.

Her success with the company was neither an accident nor a forgone conclusion. Mildred was very intentional with her actions and performance. Because of her hard work, she was very successful. She is very responsible professional, and pleasant.

No one on the team is surprised when they hear that Mildred has been retained.

*Story: Samuel*

Samuel has a very different attitude toward his work. He is honest and generally pleasant. He arrives for work on time and leaves his cubicle at exactly at 5:00 p.m. each night.

His work product is acceptable but rarely shows extra initiative or innovation. He considers work and the rest of his life as two separate things. This has led to no additional time spent socializing or networking within the company. He is not known by anyone in a higher position than his immediate supervisor.

Samuel receives satisfactory evaluations but is not identified for advancement.

Samuel's interview also takes a short period of time. He is identified by his rather average performance and his marginal contributions. He is told that he will be released at the end of the month.

Both Mildred and Samuel determined their own fate by the way they viewed their work and the effort they demonstrated. People who really like their work are willing to commit to longer hours and harder work to accomplish a team goal or for the betterment of the company. They understand the interdependency they share with their employers. They have developed a career. They have *branded* themselves by their choices.

Samuel's performance reflected a person who saw his employment as separate from himself. His self-imposed isolation and failure to network harmed his *brand*. He treated his work as just a job and gave only what was required.

The great hope is that Samuel will realize why he was not retained and turn this current disappointment into a proactive method of seeking solid input, guidance, and coaching. If this disappointment is used as a positive building block, he will be able to be much more effective in his next endeavor.

Samuel has two choices: he can change or remain the same. He has the ability to determine his future. He can chose to be a valued associate that no one would ever want to lose, or he can remain an *at-risk employee*.

So how did Mildred and Samuel react to the news?

Mildred was grateful and professional. She kept the decision to herself to avoid any insensitivity toward the feelings of those who were being released.

Samuel showed his anger quite openly. He slammed his notebook on the table and immediately went to another associate's desk to share the bad news. He said it was unfair and arbitrary. He told his coworker that he had done everything the company had asked of him. He deserved to be retained. He blamed his immediate supervisor for not liking him and never letting him excel. He mumbled about a discrimination lawsuit as he left early for the day.

You all know people like Mildred and Samuel. Neither is a bad person. Neither is dishonest or unreliable. Each has made a choice about his or her work life.

Unfortunately, you see far too many people acting and thinking like Samuel. As soon as he heard something he did not like, he started the *blame game.* He sought to excuse his performance by passing the blame to anyone other than himself. He never looked at the *cause and effect* of his situation. If he had, he would have realized that the way he conducted himself put him in a very weak position for employment retention.

Some people play the *blame game* all the time. To avoid the *blame game* and take personal responsibility, I offer you the five *f*'s.

## The Five *F*'s—A Leadership Process

The first *f* represents *fouling up*.

You are only human, so you are going to make mistakes. You are going to *foul up*, probably a minimum of once a day. The key is to learn from your mistakes.

Once you have *fouled up,* a responsible person will immediately *fess up*.

Because of embarrassment, not wanting to be wrong, or not wanting to face the consequences of their actions, many people immediately try to deflect the *foul up* onto someone or something else. They begin the *blame game*.

They go into denial about the *foul up*, saying things like the following:

- "It's no big deal."
- "Nobody got hurt."
- "Somebody did the same thing to me, so payback is okay."
- "Everybody was doing it, so I thought it was okay."

This list can go on and on. Take a few minutes to list the excuses you personally use to try to distance yourself from a problem that you created. Excuse making does not relieve you of the responsibility to *fix it*.

Avoiding, the *blame game* and excuse making will give you credibility with others. It does not remove the consequences of your actions, but it does show that you take responsibility for your actions and are willing to resolve the issue.

The second *f* is *fessing up*.

Now that the *foul up* has been identified, the person who caused the problem has *fessed up*. It is now time to *fix it*.

The third *f* is for *fixing it*.

The most important characteristic of this stage is the fix needs to be completed by the person who *fouled up*. It is not the responsibility of parents, siblings, employees, or superiors. This step is critical in the learning process of the person who made the mistake. If the originator can defer his or her problem to someone else, he or she will learn nothing. This creates a pattern of dependency on others to fix his or her messes.

The fourth *f* is *forgetting about it*.

My son added the fourth *f*. Apparently, he thought I was not very good at this step. He was correct. Once the *foul up* has been identified, *fessed up*, and *fixed*, it is time to put it behind you.

It is astounding the number of people who have carried the guilt or the harm of a *foul up* for years. It can destroy relationships, careers, and marriages. Holding on to issues of the past is a very unhealthy behavior.

The fifth and final *f* is *forgiveness*.

It is important to understand that *forgiveness* benefits the forgiver far more than the person who may have caused the harm. Forgiving will allow you to clean your emotional slate to prevent scarring future interactions with residual negative emotions.

Before we move on, lets recap the five *f*'s:

1. *Fouling up* is a daily occurrence for everyone.
2. *Fessing up* is taking responsibility for your actions.
3. *Fixing it helps* you find true resolution and imbeds a learning element within you.
4. *Forgetting about it* allows you to move on.
5. *Forgiveness* clears the emotional slate to the benefit of future experiences,

## Examples of the Five *F*'s

*A Personal Story*

I was a senior executive in an office with approximately forty associates. As with many such offices, we had a small kitchen for the use of all our associates. It became an ongoing challenge to have each kitchen user clean up after him- or herself.

One day I went into the kitchen with a few coffee cups that had been pushed aside on my conference table. When I walked these dirty dishes into the kitchen, I placed them in the dishwasher and began a search for the dishwashing detergent.

Finding no granular detergent, I decided to use a liquid alternative. You probably already see my big mistake. I turned on the dishwasher and returned to my office.

About a half hour later, I heard a shriek from the direction of the kitchen. Fearing that someone had been hurt, I jumped to my feet and went to investigate. Standing in the doorway of the kitchen was my executive assistant. She was examining the nearly knee-high sea of soap bubbles that covered the entire kitchen floor. It actually looked like snow!

She immediately knew the cause of the problem. She blamed it on another associate who was very forgetful and often caused small issues around the office.

Her yell rallied the attention of everyone in the office. Everybody ran to the kitchen to give assistance.

I immediately confessed that I had *fouled up*. Several people snickered, making me feel a little foolish.

My executive assistant immediately tried to take me off the hot seat by saying it may have been her fault for not purchasing more granular dishwashing supplies.

I appreciated her attempt to cover for the big guy, but I reaffirmed my ownership of the problem. In other words, I *fessed up*.

Several people began to clean up. They did not think it was the job of the boss to clean the bubbles from the floor.

I stopped them and thanked them for their help. I reminded them about the five *f*'s, which we had used as the foundation for our interoffice relationships. I reminded them that I had *fouled up*, *fessed up*, and now it was my responsibility to *fix it*.

For the next forty-five minutes I removed the bubbles and washed the floor. When I finished, I rallied everyone to the kitchen to see the results. They were in awe. The floor shined like never before. We all marveled that what we had thought was an off-white floor was actually bright white.

After the expected joking, I asked everyone to return to his or her desk. I also reminded them that they now had to *forget about it*, followed by *forgive*.

Unfortunately, they were not very good at forgetting about it. By the end of the week, everyone in the world knew about my mistake. They also knew I had lived up to the principles of the five *f*'s by cleaning the mess up myself.

The way they provided forgiveness was a note to me, signed by the associates, that said I was relieved from any kitchen cleanup responsibilities in the future,

No one is exempt from the five *f*'s.

## The F-Word

*Forgiveness: removing yourself and others from past transgressions*

It is incredible how very long and how intensely human beings hold on to sins, mistakes, and foolish acts of the past. Some poor individuals never recover from a romantic rejection, an unfair business result, or sibling jealousy. Their entire lives are tainted by their inability to face a problem and then move on.

Forgiveness is the core of most religions, as well as a critical step in all psychological healing. The remarkable fact is that forgiveness benefits the forgiver far more than the person being forgiven.

Forgiving some wrong that has been done against you releases you to venture out and enjoy new, unblemished experiences. It allows you to learn how harmful some acts can be so you can avoid inflicting them on others.

Forgiveness is the first step to compassion. Harboring negative feelings is self-destructive and affects a person's health and mental state of mind.

Being stubborn based on a conviction that you are right or believing someone really did you wrong becomes a festering ache that pulls your life and spirit down. It often negatively impacts the people around you as well.

Learn from your pain. Let it become a new road map to releasing hurtful things or feelings.

Forgiveness is liberating for both the forgiver and the forgiven.

## Timeless Wisdom

*Everyone is responsible for his or her own actions and results.*

Choices separate people. Good choices generally have positive outcomes. Bad choices lead to disaster.

When one prisoner in the penitentiary asked his fellow prisoner what he had done to be sent to prison, the fellow prisoner's response was, "Bad judgment. Repeated bad judgment." The first prisoner said he was there for the exact same reason.

You are totally responsible for your actions and their consequences. You always have the ability to choose.

---

*"Don't become rigid and tense, ready to do battle. Never oppose that which opposes you. Don't oppose, compose."*

*(Neal Donald Walsch)*

---

Remain composed and relaxed. You will receive what you need at the right time and the right way. Find an opportunity in every experience.

Accept your present realities but never believe them to be permanent or unchangeable.

Evolve with every opportunity.

*Integrity is another way to match motive with action.*

There is a great expression in business and politics: follow the money. This creates a trail that exposes the motive for any action or lack of action. Once you make the link between an action and the motive for that action, you can easily determine the integrity of the person in question.

Motive reveals all.

# Building Consensus and Leadership

**M**any great books have been written about the dramatic difference between a leader and a manager. One of the most critical differences is that a leader will build and maintain consensus with the members of a team. This is much more complex and difficult than it might appear to the casual observer.

Let's diligently explore leadership, consensus building, management, individual empowerment, measuring outcomes, and teamwork.

## Leaders and Leadership

Not all people have the personal characteristics to lead. Individuals are not born to be leaders; generally, current leaders mentor them. They learn the leadership skills of others. They are individuals who are willing to take on greater responsibilities, exercise sound judgment, have a moral compass, and can understand how the small details influence the big picture.

---

*The quality of a leader is reflected in the standards they set for themselves.*

—Ray Kroc, founder of McDonalds

---

Leaders project a caring, compassionate aura in times of challenge. They are the people who often make grave individual sacrifices for the benefit of many. They lead because they have inadvertently or intentionally earned the respect and admiration of those who choose to follow them.

They also radiate a charisma that draws others to them. People believe what they say because of the confidence they display. They often do not seek to take point in a time of need; others who admire and trust them push them to the forefront.

Leaders are not limited by ethnicity, age, gender, physical stature, or intelligence. Others quickly recognize them during trying times when their true traits come to the surface. Several notable historic leaders come immediately to mind:

- George Washington
- Abraham Lincoln
- Winston Churchill
- Dr. Martin Luther King
- Mother Theresa
- Mahatma Gandhi

---

*The real leader has no need to lead ... he is content to point the way.*
—Henry Miller

---

If it were not for the conditions during the times in which they lived and their decisions to take personal risks to help mankind, these names would mean very little to the general public.

Leaders have a purpose: - creating passion around an important issue that they are willing to sacrifice dearly to accomplish. Yet, with all that said, leaders are the servants to the many. They take the ridicule and the blame when things do not go as planned. They build consensus of purpose through their oratory skills, their networking, their personal commitments, their examples, and finally their personas.

Without leaders, the world would be in a state of chaos, for leaders create and organize the actions needed to achieve greatness. They inspire others whose spirits have been weakened by challenge or defeat. They are relentless in their optimism that around each corner they will find the needed strength to survive, thrive, and prosper.

Leaders understand the value of positive thinking. They can also measure the destructive impact of negative thoughts, words, and deeds. They truly understand the theory of *cause and effect.* They know that whatever you *cause* to happen will have consequences, which we call *effect.*

They understand that this is a universal law that cannot be avoided.

Leaders build trust! They sincerely understand both the importance and the potential consequences of telling and following the truth. They also know that when they no longer hold the trust of the people they serve, they no longer have any value as a leader.

Our perception of leadership has diminished over the last decade because of the full transparency of our evolving society. Leaders can be caught on video and audio devices in almost any circumstance. Every e-mail, memo, tweet, quote, etc., can be saved forever.

Words, deeds, and promises are archived forever. They are easily accessible, and it's easy to compare promises with actual actions and results. Scandals, abuses, and indulgences are revealed daily about the people we once admired.

Since leaders are not perfect, they will make mistakes. They will err because of their human frailties and weakness.

The easiest way to measure the quality of a leader is to evaluate his or her motives.

Ask yourself if the decisions made by the leader were universally beneficial or self-serving. Were the reasons or motivations for personal gain or for the true benefit of others?

Ask if the decisions made caused unintended consequences or were made with poor judgment or a lack of attention to important details.

---

*Do the hard jobs first. The easy jobs will take care of themselves.*
—Dale Carnegie

---

Ask if the leader was making a decision out of ego or for the general good of others.

Ask if the leader is acting from raw emotion or a position of calm resolve.

Applaud the calculated risks taken by a well-intended leader, regardless of the outcome, when the motive was intended for the benefit of others.

## The Key Test of Leadership

True leaders cannot lead without integrity. If their integrity has been compromised, all of their decisions will be questioned and viewed as potentially suspicious. This causes those they lead to hesitate or balk, losing the advantage of the *moment.*

Shared leadership is ideal, but unfortunately it seems to be refuted by the human experience. In all groups, a single person is needed to unite the interest of many. This leader is not a dictator but a *consensus builder.* This person is the one individual who needs to maintain the focus of the group without getting ensnared in the emotions of personal interest. This person needs to encourage lively and diverse debate, followed by a call to action.

The number of other effective leaders a person develops boldly measures his or her true leadership excellence. Developing future leaders is a legacy of success.

---

*The creation of a thousand forests is in one acorn.*
—Ralph Waldo Emerson

---

Leaders tend to be generalists. They have a rare innate ability to create and see the vision that will drive the needed action. They sense what is needed to achieve the desired goal. They motivate and enable people to clearly understand the end goal and the contribution of each team member in the process. They spend their time observing, not judging, always on the lookout for better ways to achieve the desired results. They must know what is going on without being intrusive or doing the work themselves. They must know that empowered people do exceptional things. Repressed people only do what they are told and become lost when the leader is not present.

---

*Never tell people how to do things. Tell them what to do and they will surprise you with their ingenuity.*
—George Patton

---

Good leaders work behind the scene like the director of a play. They are responsible for all of the elements of the performance and are never seen by the audience. They allow the performers to receive all of the praise. They bask in the knowledge that without all of their invisible actions, the show wouldn't go on!

Leadership is lonely and stressful. Being a great leader, you may only be in the spotlight a few times, but you will experience being in the doghouse daily. The reward of leadership is having significantly contributed to a lofty endeavor for the betterment of others.

---

*When an effective leader is finished with his or her work, the people say it happened naturally.*

–Lao Tsu

---

Leaders influence the very emotions and the feelings of others. They hire or secure skilled managers to carry out the details and get the actual work done.

Leaders surround themselves with experts and managers to determine the necessary details to bring the vision to life.

## Examples of Leadership

---

*The only thing we have to fear is fear itself!*

–Franklin D. Roosevelt

---

The historical statement above was one of the most important leadership utterances of World War II. This statement was made by the leader of the U.S. and projected a sense of calm resolve and optimism in an attempt to replace the negative thoughts and fears of a country under fire. No details were given as to the number of new planes built or how the situation would be resolved. The message was designed to appeal to the emotions of the populace and to reassure the citizens that U.S. leadership was confident in a victory over Nazi Germany, Italy, and Japan.

Leaders need to inspire and speak the truth, laced with optimistic sentiment, to raise the morale and resolve of listeners. Their every comment must be uttered with enthusiasm, which conveys the conviction of truth.

FOUND TREASURE

Great leaders know that realism must be the foundation of the message. They understand both the good and bad consequences of their actions.

Great leaders have and must display a *can-do attitude*, supported by persistent and positive affirmations about the necessary journey and the importance of success.

Leaders define what success looks like. They paint a clear picture of what is being sought, the role of others in attaining the goal, and the real benefits to all. Leaders never mistake effort for results. Trying does not replace doing.

---

*The first responsibility of a leader is to define reality. The last is to say thank you.*

—Max DePree

---

A leader who is untrustworthy cannot aspire to great deeds or sustainable results. He or she is simply managing a situation until a true leader is found.

Leaders are respected for their vision and their courage. They are willing to make hard decisions in the face of challenging circumstances. They remain very calm when others panic. They understand the true value of a well-thought-out plan versus an irrational reaction.

Leaders do not run into battles, but they never back away when one is needed. They never start a fight, but they do finish them.

Leaders are very highly valued because they must be responsible for all the good and the bad results of their actions. They must openly admit their errors with a firm commitment to avoid similar errors in the future.

---

*You can't build a reputation on what you are going to do.*

—Henry Ford

---

Leaders also must separate themselves from their peers in order to make difficult and complicated decisions that are often necessary, devoid of the potential distraction of personal entanglements. They transfer energy to others, which is why they age much more quickly than their peers. They accept the stress and isolation so that they might be fair, objective, and assertive.

Being a leader is the loneliest role for a good leader is the servant of the people he or she is sworn to serve. When personal gain becomes more important than the collective benefit of the many people served, the leader is rendered impotent. Self-serving motives truly expose would-be leaders as frauds.

Compare the differences between a public servant and a politician. A public servant does his or her job to help the people. Politicians often seek office to personally benefit from the power they have over others.

Leaders are easy to spot. They inspire others to great accomplishments. When you meet a true, gifted leader, be grateful, for there are many imposters posing as leaders, hoping you won't notice.

## Managing versus Leading

Management is a hierarchal designation of an individual who has been given responsibility for a specific product or result to be achieved by workers he or she supervises.

The employer, or leader, appoints managers often based on tenure or experience.

Managers are skilled in the specific details of executing the work needed to accomplish the goal. They are often not experienced or skilled in building team consensus. Instead, they rely on hierarchical authority.

The achievements of the manager's subordinates are usually determined by performance reviews, with the reward being continued employment.

Poor performance is often addressed with job demotion or termination.

Managers determine the tasks that need to be completed to achieve the desired outcome. They delegate specific job responsibilities to each individual within the work team. The manager then supervises the performance of each individual.

Individual workers rely exclusively on the manager for specific directives, timelines, decisions, and results. Individual empowerment is rarely given or expected.

To manage someone or something, a person is given the charge of executing the responsibilities or details that will lead to the successful completion of the job. The manager himself or herself may not be involved in setting the project vision. He or she may be delegated the task of simply completing specific functions without an understanding of how those functions contribute to the final goal.

Managers do not require charisma to complete their functions. They may not generate collaboration or team support to achieve the team objective. They primarily supervise the doers.

Managers selected based on tenure only may lack the personal skills to receive the maximum effort from the members of their teams. They do not need to explain the intricate reasons for the work that needs to be done. They continuously give orders, measure expected results, and evaluate performance.

A good leader often makes a very poor manager. A good manager does not always become a good leader. Both roles have very separate functions that require different skill sets.

When a person attempts to perform both roles, a leader and a manager, he or she is dramatically compelled to wear two very different hats at all times. This is one of the major reasons a company organized in this way fails or is limited in its ability to grow.

The leader-manager is trying to be both the visionary and the primary performer of the endeavor.

Can some people successfully manage and lead at the same time? Of course. There are always exceptions. But as the enterprise grows, these two responsibilities rarely coexist in one individual.

So it is very important that a person building a team or a business knows when it is time to evolve from being a doer to being a leader of doers.

*Story: Tony the Barber*

Tony migrated to the Unites States from Italy with very little money in his pocket. He came to America to seek an opportunity to raise his family and start his own business. His desire to succeed was his greatest asset.

He worked for three years loading freight onto railroad cars. The work was physically demanding. He would return home at the end of a shift exhausted and in pain.

Tony and his family lived a very basic lifestyle. There were no luxuries. He took most of the money he had to the bank to save up for the day he could start his own business.

An opportunity presented itself to him one day. For a price he could afford, Tony could lease a very small barbershop. After conferring with his wife, he decided he would take the plunge. He rented the shop and changed the sign on the small window to read "Tony's Barber Shop."

In the beginning, business was very slow. People did not know Tony or his skills. Gradually, men came in to get their hair cut and found Tony, one barber chair, three waiting room chairs, and a very small table with free coffee for customers.

Tony's personality created a friendly atmosphere in which stories and joking were plentiful. He loved what he was doing!

Happy customers recommended Tony's place to their friends. Often customers who didn't need a haircut would drop in just to say hi and visit. They loved the friendly environment that Tony had created. This is when the problems began.

As Tony's business grew, he had to increase the number of haircuts he did each day to meet the ever growing customer demand. His ability to visit with customers and inquire about their personal lives, families, and jobs diminished. He had to hurry his work to simply keep up with the customer volume. The stale coffee went cold, the stories got old, and the joking all but stopped.

Tony's income had grown nicely for the first year, but he started to see his income growth level off as the number of daily haircuts maxed out. To raise his income, he would have to raise his prices, which would send many of his customers to the competition. If he stayed at the current status quo, he would have serious health issues because of his long hours and growing stress.

The happy Tony who in the early days of the shop had come home energized and optimistic about the future had transformed into a exhausted man who was almost bitter about his circumstances. He loved the stories, the coffee, and the visits with customers, all of which he was rapidly losing because the business was now controlling him rather than him controlling the business. Tony really liked cutting hair. He got a great deal of satisfaction from seeing his customers looking sharp and confident. He especially loved to give a future bridegroom a free haircut and a shave the day before his wedding. He would always present his bill with the following statement: "No charge today! Be happy." Signed Tony.

One day Tony started having pains in his chest. He was unable to stand. He had to be physically assisted by several customers who wisely called an ambulance. Tony had suffered a mild heart attack. He was released from the hospital after a few days with orders from his doctor to lose at least fifty pounds. While Tony was in the hospital, his one-man barbershop remained closed. Customers who had normally just dropped by for a haircut had no alternative but to go to a local competitor. On top of incurring some rather hefty medical bills, Tony's income disappeared during his recovery.

Tony realized during his recuperation that he was at a crossroads within his business and career. He knew he could not continue to do business or live the way he had in the past. His personal crisis demanded that he make risky changes.

He drew up a detailed plan of action. He went to his landlord and rented additional space so he could expand the shop. He recruited friends and customers to aid him in designing the new shop. He added three more barber chairs and expanded the waiting room. He installed a larger coffee machine. He got several sports and men's magazines. He installed a moderate-sized television that would remain constantly fixed to a sport's channel. He made a comfortable environment so his customers would feel at home.

He posted the "joke of the day" on a board so customers could bring cartoons or a joke to share.

Next, Tony put an advertisement in the local newspapers for qualified barbers. He would rent them a chair and then take a percentage of each service the individual barbers performed. He also rented out his chair so he could spend more time managing the business, talking to customers, and taking time off to exercise.

Tony had evolved and so had his business. He began to make more money. He recreated the atmosphere he wanted for the shop. He had a life outside of work that allowed him time to take care of himself and spend time with his family.

His most favorite part of the business was giving each customer a special comb that sported the saying, "Have no care while we cut your hair at Tony's Place."

### Lesson Learned

Tony was forced by his circumstances to transition from being a doer-manager to a leader of doers. This required Tony to develop brand new skill sets in accounting, advertising, sales, business management, personnel management, capital public relations, etc.

*After Story*

Eventually Tony's original shop could no longer serve all of the customers who desired his services. He had to learn the skill of duplicating himself so he could open shop number two and then number three and so on.

From a simple beginning, Tony built a small empire of barbershops that he could be proud to call Tony's.

Let's look at the steps Tony had to take to be successful. While you read these details, apply them to your own life and your present situation. Realize that every thought, word, and action is creative. Some people think a lot and do nothing. Some people say plenty but then slide into easier and less productive habits. Some people see that the needed action is too demanding. Tony had all of these challenges, but he persevered. Why?

- When he had the thought of starting his own business, he stood up.
- While standing, he started to walk.
- When he decided what he really wanted to do and took action, his passion turned his walk into a run.
- Once he started to have success, he converted his sprint into a marathon.
- When he completed the marathon, he turned it into a positive lifestyle.

## Beware of Self-Serving Leaders

There are many quotes and common sense sayings that explain being trustworthy and truthful.

"Walk the talk."

"Never make a contract your body can't keep."

"Say what you mean and mean what you say."

*Truthfulness* has often become a fleeting value for a large segment of our society. Many people have been pushed to a level of skepticism. Before telling the truth, many people calculate the potential consequences.

Some individuals are so self-absorbed that they think they are better than the common man, which allows them to take whatever action, no matter how heinous, to advance their self-interest.

They generally talk a great game with lots of smack talk and boasting but little evidence or action to back up their grand claims.

They are all about winning. Stretching the truth or lying are unimportant as long as they get their way. Rules are simply to be ignored. Guidelines are altered to support their personal motives.

*Perhaps the less we have, the more we are required to brag.*
—John Steinbeck, *East of Eden*

They turn a deaf ear to the ideas, opinions, and needs of others. These are simply obstacles to be avoided. They are right, despite any evidence to the contrary.

They are so prideful that even when proven wrong or out of step, they will conclude that they need to *insist and persist* with their original plan of action.

They build relationships only when those relationships can benefit their personal agendas. They sever these alliances immediately after attaining their goals.

They have very short memories about those who help them, but they harbor personal grudges for a lifetime. They consider people who are agreeable as merely weak or stupid. They can be used as tools to accomplish these self-serving leaders' desired goals.

When a mistake is made, these individuals immediately make excuses to remove themselves from any and all responsibility. They spin their words to confuse the facts but always agree with the criticizer that something should be done to rectify the situation. They often make wild promises that they know they cannot keep just to quiet the moment.

No lie is too big or excuse too grand to remain outside the circle of responsibility.

*The price of greatness is responsibility.*
—Winston Churchill

They lack any awareness about the attitudes, needs, and feelings of others. They sincerely believe they're always right, so perceived lesser people should be happy to be in their presence.

They are masters of disguise. They smile at you while smothering you

111

with compliments clearly to advance their personal agenda. They truly do not understand or care why people hate them or why they have a very limited number of loyal friends.

They are *toxic people* to be avoided at all cost. If you get between them and their self-appointed importance, you will be sacrificed for the good of their advancement.

Trust is something a person must constantly earn, and it must be demonstrated on a regular basis.

---

*The trust of the innocent is the liar's most useful tool.*

—Steven King

---

Consistently being truthful makes a person trustworthy. When his or her personal interest is challenged with the betterment of others, the person's actions remain righteous no matter the consequences.

Once trust is lost, it is rarely restored. The pain of lies and deceitful action remain as a bitter reminder that when the person in question is tempted again, the trust will again be violated. No matter how much a person excuses his or her actions or claims innocence, past behavior labels him or her suspect.

The way we measure the trustworthiness of people is how they perform after making a mistake. Do they stand up and admit wrongdoing? Do they blame their actions on other people, reasons, or circumstances? Do they understand the penalties for their actions?

Integrity is a tricky lifetime achievement. Living by a set of standards or values that help you navigate your life actions is extremely important. The very unpopular nature of your belief will draw opposition from some and harm from others. A get-along attitude may be the simplest and most immediate response, but it can create problems in future experiences.

---

*Trust is the glue of life. It's the most essential ingredient in effective communication. It's the foundational principle that holds all relationships.*

—Stephen Covey

---

It takes incredible courage to stand up and be counted. It proclaims your value and place in the world. While some rationalize why they withhold action and quietly withdraw, others will make a statement of who they really are by pressing on to victory.

Be very proud of those who stand on their beliefs, even though others think them shortsighted or foolish.

These are decisions that haunt every human being. Will they act in accordance with what they believe is right or decide to wrongfully act for personal gain or to conform to the will of others?

You can always measure the self-interest of a person by examining his or her motive for taking or not taking action. Does the motive benefit them or others? Does the action or lack of action harm someone?

## The F-Word

*Fear: the roadblock to success and happiness*

The greatest single emotional characteristic that prevents personal evolution, happiness, or success is fear. All negativity in life comes from fear.

The vast majority of your imagined or anticipated fear will never find reality. It seems ridiculous to waste your life worrying about the unlikely. Live without anxiety by remaining in the moment and staying calm.

Looking at your fear will often rob it of its imagined severity, probability, and pain. Replace fear with truths or knowledge. Remove the myth, and replace it with the confidence that you will be provided the tools necessary to adapt to every challenge; this will turn each fear into an opportunity.

---

*Anger is FEAR declared.*
*Depression is FEAR suppressed.*
—Neal Donald Walsch

---

Negative thoughts are powerfully destructive.

---

*Negativity happens when you want something you do not have or*
*you have something you do not want.*
—Neal Donald Walsch

---

Fear is created by what-if and why questions. Remember, awareness mobilizes; fear paralyzes.

# Timeless Wisdom

*Collaborate, do not dominate.*

"Who made you boss?" "You do not own me." These are the kind of questions or statements that surface when an individual appoints him- or herself as the leader of a group. As the group gathers, a natural leader who the majority of the group members can support will appear. The group may decide that there is no need for an individual leader by creating subgroups on critical elements of the project that may reap greater results.

Listen to all and find merit in their thoughts.

*True leadership cannot lead from behind.*

Sitting behind at a safe distance from the fight sends a message to others that the leader is not willing to make a personal commitment and lead by example. Leaders who inspire lead from the front. Leaders ask people to follow them, not precede them.

Show what you believe by being in the lead.

*Walk in another man's shoes.*

This is the greatest awareness tool that anyone can employ when dealing with others. Speaking constantly from an "I" position does not allow you to relate to the emotions of others.

Reverse your thinking for greater benefits. Rather than thinking from your position, embrace what might be the conditions and emotions of the other person.

Try this method: When you have a challenging situation that needs understanding from both involved parties, simply switch seats and take on the role of the other person. Let him or her also role-play as if he or she were you.

Can I try your shoes on for size?

# Balancing Priorities

It is imperative that you create a meaningful circle of advisors, personal friends, and mentors if you intend to maximize your life experiences. We're all endowed with different strengths and weaknesses. Our imperfect state of being requires that we offer our strengths to others in exchange for the skills we lack.

This is called the *bartering of knowledge.*

This is a critical human need. You intuitively know you are more powerful and much more successful when you gather diverse talents and opinions to develop a plan, thought, etc.

---

*Action expresses priorities.*

—Mahatma Gandhi

---

You accumulate knowledge every moment of your life. Experience is the primary educator of both the young and old. Knowledge becomes wisdom when you have experienced a broad array of life lessons. This is the very reason cultures revere their elders: they have the experience to make seasoned and wise choices.

## Example of Balance and Flexibility

Have you ever passed a park in the wee hours of the morning and seen a few people practicing the art of tai chi. It is exercise mixed with meditation that is focused on joining the mind, body, and spirit through ritualistic movements of balance and flexibility.

Think about that for a moment. No one can function in an ever-changing world without maintaining a balance of all of his or her earthly demands. Neither can anyone function at a high level if he or she lacks the flexibility to adapt to constant change.

As you get older, the balance between the mind, body, and soul and your ability to cope with the fluctuations of life will play a huge role in your longevity and enjoyment of life. You must continually make a series of minor daily adjustments to lead you to your desired destination.

You and the rest of the world admire the courageous individuals who have the ability to survive the rigorous training to become fighter pilots. Only the very best can achieve this goal. Their qualities are both numerous and admirable. However, they use the modern equipment available to them to ensure their results. The computers placed in the modern-day fighter planes are remarkable but not perfect. The human element is needed to make minor navigational adjustments so that the plane can reach the desired destination.

As a human, you also need to make adjustments along the way to enhance your skills, performance, and life experience. This process is never complete. That is why you must always be in search of new experiences and accomplishments.

*The key is not to prioritize what's on your schedule, but to schedule your priorities.*

—Stephen Covey

## The Process of Adjustment

Change requires courage. It pushes you from the known to the unknown. Constant change is a fundamental law of the universe. It can be delayed, but it cannot be avoided. Make a personal assessment of your life and profession to make the needed adjustments for a more productive and fulfilling life.

- Identify possible areas of needed focus.
- Network among individuals with the skills to support your goal.

- Research legal requirements and restrictions related to your goal.
- Identify personal and institutional resources to support your goal.
- Create a timeline of needs, details, and completion dates.
- Create a model to use when presenting your idea, thought, or goal.
- Realize that success is the outcome of a well-defined developmental process.

Skipping steps in the process will often cause some completion delays or create necessary adjustments in the future.

Since most of us are limited in our areas of expertise, it is advisable to create a support team of competent and equally committed experts. Below you see a very simple example of the obvious need and great value of gathering experts into your circle of confidence.

## FAMILY MAN OR WOMAN

## PHYSICIAN- DENTIST-INSURANCE ADVISOR -BANKER

These are the typical advisors that most people have. But wait. Aren't there a lot more?

## MINISTER OR SPIRITUAL ADVISOR-
## INVESTMENT ADVISOR-TEACHER
## MENTOR-ACCOUNTANT-AUTO MECHANIC-
## COMPUTER EXPERT-COACH

Each of these experts contributes to your personal well-being. They are gathered around you to handle specific details in your life that demand their particular skills. They are not to determine your life journey; they are simply in your life to handle the daily circumstances that need attention.

They can simplify your life to give you the freedom and the time to pursue the expansion and achievement of your life purpose.

Their diverse opinions, ideas, and advice provide you with knowledge that will allow you to select the correct options necessary to support your personal life journey.

Adding their input and expertise to the influence of your family, friends, environment, etc., you develop your vision of the world and your role in it.

## Intellectual Groups

To explore great thoughts and ideas and turn them into reality, it is important for any would-be entrepreneur to collaborate with individuals who are open-minded, innovative, creative, clever, and collaborative thinkers. Collectively, these positive and innovative thinkers can overcome insurmountable obstacles while prevailing in unchartered or dangerous waters. One of the greatest minds of the industrial revolution was that of Thomas Edison. He created well over one thousand patented inventions during his lifetime. His greatest traits were that of patience and inexhaustible persistence.

Even with his imaginative mind, he sought out the great thinkers of his time to share his ideas. He met regularly with auto giants Henry Ford and Harvey Firestone to think impossible dreams, speak about futuristic endeavors, and create grand plans of action.

*Coming together is a beginning; keeping together is progress; working together is success.*

—Henry Ford

Pessimists were not invited to join their ranks. Though they clearly understood the potential challenges they might face, they remained *possibility thinkers.*

They simply dared to dream! Then they turned those dreams into reality.

These innovators changed the world. They set the stage for future dreamers like Bill Gates, Martin Luther King, Steve Jobs, Mother Teresa, Warren Buffet, etc.

*If you think you can do a thing or think you can't do a thing, you're right.*

—Henry Ford

You know the names of the innovators who persisted through challenges and tedious work, as well as leaders without limited vision. None of us know the many names of the dreamers who saw their dreams as too small or difficult so they simply let them die from lack of nourishment.

---

*Don't find fault, find a remedy.*

—Henry Ford

---

It is not enough to simply have creative ideas.

These thoughts will likely remain meaningless without the *passion of action.*

## Your Legacy

Your legacy will be the sum total of your contribution to the betterment of your fellow human beings, whether that's in the world of business, social change, personal development, or spiritual advancement.

It is not imperative that your name appear in the history books of tomorrow, but it is very important that your life be more than a continuous process of taking without giving back.

The greatest American industrialists who accumulated tremendous wealth found abbreviated satisfaction in merely earning great riches. Most desired to celebrate their good fortune by becoming philanthropists. They gave of their wealth to schools and universities, medical research, and programs for the underprivileged. They were blessed with success, so they shared it with others. Those who simply coveted their good fortune often left no memory of their earthly walk.

You have the joyful ability to write your own plan and determine your own destiny. Your legacy will be born of your dreams, thoughts, actions, and giving.

It is your time to cast your fate to the wind, to dream the grandest thoughts, to tackle the biggest obstacles, and to be the best you that you can possibly imagine.

Tony, the humble barber, reached for the stars out of desperation, but he achieved so much for the effort. He provided a wonderful living for his family. He employed literally hundreds of people, who were able to support their families. He served as a role model to others with limited means, demonstrating how to be very successful through hard work, adaptation to change, and creating a brand based on fairness, quality, and honesty.

## Your Brand

Each individual has created his or her *brand* through his or her words and actions. Over time, the brand and the person become one. Unfortunately, most people never really reflect on their *brand*. Neither do they compare their *brand* with the perception of others.

*Story: Confidence versus Reservation*

Henry doesn't seem very confident in himself most of the time. He rarely combs his hair and is not concerned about his general appearance. He is quiet and reserved and simply appears to go with the flow most of the time.

Gabby is a member of the girl's basketball team. She was voted team captain by the other players. She is a solid student who enjoys being a writer and editor for the school newspaper. She takes pride in her appearance, although she is not prone to wearing the latest fashion craze. She interacts well with others, both in her own age group and adults. She aspires to attend a good college to get a teaching degree. Gabby loves to dance. She is known to be up for anything fun.

How would you describe Gabby's brand? Mark all that apply. Now do the same for Henry.

| GABBY | BRAND ITEM | HENRY |
|---|---|---|
| | A loner | |
| | Moody | |
| | Emotionally well-balanced | |
| | A leader | |
| | A leader | |
| | A loser | |
| | Snobbish | |
| | Happy | |
| | Shy | |
| | Enthusiastic | |
| | Intelligent | |
| | Popular | |
| | A team player | |
| | Attractive to the opposite sex | |

Which person would you hire for a position and why?

> *A brand for a company is like a reputation for a person. You earn reputation by trying to do hard things well.*
>
> —Jeff Bezos

Everything you say and do is a statement of who you are. In other words, your *brand* is made and maintained by the way you act and present yourself to others. When your *brand* is not consistent with the way others perceive you, there is clearly a major disconnect that screams for some introspection.

> *Master your strengths, outsource your weaknesses.*
>
> —Ryan Kahn

When you are acting in a way that is not consistent with what you think of yourself, you need to reaffirm who you want to be and adjust your behavior accordingly. The great news is that you always have the ability to change yourself whenever you desire. You have the ability to adapt to the ever-changing stages in life. This is what is known as *the process of evolution.* It is inescapable and natural.

## Life Stages

- Infancy (preschool)
- Childhood (grade school)
- Adolescence (middle school)
- Young adult (high school)
- Young professional (college)
- Young family (marriage)
- Middle age (marriage or empty nest)
- Pre-retirement (pre-senior and tenured)
- Retirement (senior)
- Elder statesperson

> *You don't stop laughing when you grow old, you grow old when you stop laughing.*
>
> —George Bernard Shaw

Think of all the phases and stages you will go through in your life. Each will come with its own set of challenges, experiences, and discoveries. Your next phase of life builds on the previous stages, providing you experience, knowledge, and wisdom.

Keep in mind that the destination is not the reward; the reward is the journey.

## The F-Word

*Family: the primary motivation for all of your actions*
You were not intended to take your life journey alone.

The universe knows your individual life purpose, which allows it to draw to you the exact people and things you need to experience your life.

God only sends you angels. Each encounter you have has a purpose. Every person you encounter comes bearing a gift. This is especially true of your immediate family.

Families cluster together to enrich your life and to provide you with help, safety, compassion, and support. Your family helps to create the environment that will mold your character for the future adventures of daily living.

Families provide the motivation for hard work and a place to find peaceful repose, compassionate support, and learning.

Each small family group contributes to the overall family of man—the mutual support of your species and the planet you call home.

Your life is a series of promises or commitments with specific intentions serving as your guide. One of your strongest instincts is to procreate. Your natural desire to reproduce is a very critical element of the sustainable survival of our species. This instinct is your compulsion to select a mate, create offspring, and protect your family as your top priority.

*Commitment one:* You mold yourself to become a mature person who strives to experience life outside the desire for self-interest. You begin the process of being identified and selected as a suitable mate or companion by another who meets your approval.

*Commitment two:* You mutually agree with your selected partner to bond together to bring your heirs into this world.

*Commitment three*: You bring forth a child carrying DNA from both of you. This arrival totally alters your life forever. Now you have a small human being who is totally dependent on you for survival, nurturing, and love. For most, this is the greatest miracle they will experience on this earthly journey.

*Commitment four:* You choose to repeat commitment three until you have built your family.

This small unit called family creates the basis for all of your decisions, actions, and hard work. It is a great joy, responsibility, and reward.

Your family combines with other families to make the community of man. Together, as a community, you will face the numerous challenges and successes life has to offer.

*Family is the center of our universe.*

## Timeless Wisdom

*"Commit your heart and soul to your goal." (Neale Donald Walsch)*
Commit yourself deeply on any matter you believe to be of the highest priority. Without a true belief that you are doing the right thing, it is very difficult to achieve any goal.

Create a partnership between your soul and your goal.

*The journey is your reward, not the destination.*
You were brought into life to embrace each experience and evolve. Do not allow stagnation or fear to impede your progress. When you find yourself displaying some form of wisdom, pause to reflect on how many things you had to go through to find your truth.

Do not get too comfortable. It will slow, alter, or stop your evolution into a better person.

*Expediency always trumps philosophy.*
We are a world drowning in our own self-imposed rules and regulations. These rules and regulations are born from a philosophy of how things should be. When philosophy butts heads with reality, expediency takes center stage.

What do you have to do now to deal with the immediate situation, even if it conflicts with your philosophical vision of how things ought to be?

# Take a Chance to Advance

People complain about their personal predicaments as the result of what has been done *to* them rather than the natural consequences of actual choices they have made. Every person has a personalized *risk tolerance*. This risk tolerance measures a person's capacity to take a risk to advance in a profession, a relationship, or any endeavor. It hinges on his or her individual ability to see risk as the first step on the road to advancement.

---

*A life lived of choice is a life of conscious action. A life lived of chance is a life of unconscious creation.*

—Neale Donald Walsch

---

Let's look at a few examples that demonstrate different levels of risk.

## Low Risk

Low risk describes a person who normally makes decisions by attempting to eliminate all of the negative consequences that may arise from a particular decision. This process of eliminating potential negative consequences is difficult because the more you view the dark side of an issue, the more problems you uncover. The person who uses this analytical method, designed to ascertain the very best decision, is often challenged to take any risk. The

124

emotional stability and confidence of the decision maker will heavily influence the final conclusion.

Unfortunately, there are very few choices that are risk free. Those that appear risk free are generally the least progressive, which makes them very questionable.

The very process that was intended to surface the best decision often creates trepidation, which dissolves the value of making a choice.

Ultimately, the many negatives discovered by the due diligence of the risk-free explorer scares him or her from taking action.

### Story: Tom

Tom, a machine operator employed by relatively small manufacturing company, has heard numerous rumors about the closing of the factory and the dissolution of the company.

Rather than seeking reliable information about other employment opportunities that would need his skills, he resigns himself to remain in his current position. He has buried his head in the sand, assuming that his denial of the facts will alter the closure.

The fateful day finally arrives. Tom is given his pink slip and two weeks of severance pay.

He has made no contingency plans. He has no prospect of future employment. He has not planned for this by setting aside any contingency funds.

He is both scared and depressed. He is angry, blaming his former employer, the failing economy, and just bad luck for his present situation.

Tom's lack of acceptance about his faltering company allowed him to unrealistically remain comfortable without change rather than seeing the need to prepare for the inevitable.

### Story: Sue

About two years ago, Sue became engaged to her Prince Charming. Over time their relationship unraveled. They went their separate ways, leaving Sue bruised and very timid about intimate relationships.

Sue has found herself feeling very lonely. Then Sue meets Ty, who is a handsome, humorous, and smart single guy. Ty pays attention to Sue, showing a real interest in getting to know her better. Ty then asks Sue out to dinner the following week.

Sue panics at the thought of starting a new relationship that has the possibility of causing her to revisit the pain she experienced with her former lover. Rather than acting on her instincts, she declines Ty's offer by making up an obviously contrived excuse.

She gives Ty her phone number. She seriously doubts she will ever be called.

Sue has missed an opportunity because she could not take the risk of being hurt again.

Low risk individuals rarely get meaningful employment advancement, high levels of achievement, or rich, rewarding lives. They seek comfort over evolution. They become victims of their own self-imposed fears, leaving the vast majority of opportunities to others.

---

*Life begins at the end of your comfort zone.*
—Neale Donald Walsch

---

They fail to understand a few basics about life:

- Change is constant.
- Adapting to life's random and constant changes requires daily risk taking.
- The greater the risk, the greater the reward.
- Risk taking requires the confidence that you will be able to cope with and survive anything life throws at you.

Low risk individuals have settled for safe and limited experiences while shying away from any unpredictable adventures. The longer they are risk-adverse, the more entrenched they become within their own self-imposed limitations. They will also teach their children to play it safe instead of embracing the limitless opportunities of living life at full throttle.

# Moderate Risk

The moderate risk person is often on the fence about taking a risk, so he or she is not capable of taking anything other than small risks.

These individuals will attempt to make their important life decisions using a balanced process that includes evaluating both the positive and negative aspects of any potential decision. They focus more on the benefits they will receive rather than the potential negative consequences.

Moderate risk takers are willing to take risks in areas of personal expertise but fail to move forward in any area in which they are less knowledgeable.

Moderate risk takers are more futuristic in their overall thinking, envisioning what could be. They seek opportunities that motivate limited change but in specific areas only. They research the facts that will lead to their decisions and normally make their decisions within a relatively short period of time.

Once they decide, they move quickly to action. Once a decision has been made, they keep their focus on the road ahead. They see no real value in looking in the rearview mirror; however, they can experience dramatic buyer's remorse if they acted impulsively.

## The Balance Approach to Life

Moderate risk individuals accept a more balanced approach to life:

- They accept change as a life constant.
- They seek many opportunities and experiences to advance specific aspects of their lives.
- They accept the risks needed to evolve.
- They are confident with their ability to handle the outcomes of their decisions.
- They will generally rely on their feelings as the highest indicator in decision making.
- They will gladly celebrate a good decision while learning from a poor one.
- They duplicate their successes, eliminating any risks that have a history of poor results.

This group feels that they also have a moderate amount of control over their lives. They are responsible for their choices even though they may occasionally join in when others complain about their perplexing and unusual circumstances. They replace complaining with venting.

Moderate risk takers view life as a series of experiences that improve over time. They envision where they want to be in deference to where they are. They are eager to embrace technology that will move them to the next level of advancement or personal mastery.

---

*If you need to know in advance that everything will "work out" before you jump in, you'll never jump into anything. Yet "jumping in" is life's greatest excitement and its greatest adventure. Don't deny yourself that. Just go for it. Trust that life will bring you benefit no matter what happens.*

—Neale Donald Walsch

---

## Story: Bob and Mary

Mary and Bob got married when they were twenty-five years old. They both have full-time employment with the potential of solid bonuses that they can achieve at progressively higher levels each year. They recognize that the future depends on sound decision making and a willingness to make temporary sacrifices for future gain. They both have continued to take college courses that support their careers. They realize this will keep them on the cutting edge of their industries.

They also know that their performance results, skills, knowledge, positive attitudes, and relationship building abilities will heavily influence their true earning potential, future employment, and advancement opportunities.

They have been married for just two years. According to their mutually agreed upon life timeline, it appeared to be time to move from renting to owning a home.

They researched the current interest rates, home costs, locations, etc., to determine their range of options. Their research indicates that they can afford a monthly mortgage payment no greater than $1,500. This conclusion will influence the potential home location and the size.

They will have to really stretch their budget to make this move. They realize that their incomes will increase annually and there will be adequate equity growth in their new home to create a truly solid nest egg for the purchase of a larger home as their family grows.

## Bob and Mary's Plan

- *Now*: Purchase an older 1,200-square-foot home, taking advantage of the present low mortgage interest rates. They will upgrade this home over time, doing 50 percent of the work themselves.
- *Four years from now:* Have their first child.
- *Five years from now:* Sell their home and use the equity to upgrade to a larger home with about 1,700 to 2,000 square feet.
- *Six years from now:* Have child number two.
- *Ten years from now*: Use the equity from their second home sale to purchase a comparable or bigger home in an area with superior schools, since the first child will be entering the educational system.

The creation of this plan has given Bob and Mary a clear road map that leads to their desired destination. They are aware that variables will enter their lives that will possibly alter their calculated plan. They are confident they will be able to adapt to whatever develops.

They also realize they both must be willing to stretch in order for their plan to succeed. Taking a calculated risk is needed today to create opportunities in the future. They are very excited about their future prospects.

## Story: Jack and Jill

Jack and Jill know that if they ever plan to retire, they need to set aside funds that will annually increase according to the important benefits of *time, value of money,* and *compounding interest.* They learn the "Rule of 72."

---

*Caution is natural, but fear is not. Do not give in to fear, yet do not abandon caution. It is a balancing act. Caution is what causes you to look both ways before crossing the street. Fear is what keeps you frozen on the curb forever. You know the difference. You can feel it.*
—Neale Donald Walsch

---

The Rule of 72 is simple: based on the interest rate you receive on your money, you can calculate when you will double your original investment. Although it is unlikely you will receive the same interest rate each year, this formula allows you to see how the size of your interest rate determines the growth of your money.

This assumes that you take the following actions:

- invest your money in year one
- continue to get the same interest rate throughout the time period
- allow your funds to compound annually

Using the Rule of 72, Jill and Sam can determine the growth patterns of their funds.

So if they get a 2% return it will take 36 years to double their money. At 4% it takes 18 years. At 6% it takes 12 years. At 10% it takes 7.2 years.

They see it will be impossible to grow their money using traditional low interest rate vehicles such as savings accounts or certificates of deposit. They have also become aware that they have to seek investment accounts that will limit or eliminate annual tax consequences.

Jill and Sam see several realities based on these simple calculations:

- They will not increase their money by placing it in many of the traditional vehicles (saving accounts, low interest rate CDs, or any interest rate returns that are subject to taxes).
- They could invest in the stock market, but small investment amounts and the volatility of the market could be problematic.
- Real estate usually requires a 20 percent down payment and a monthly mortgage payment at the market value interest rate.
- Life insurance is something to explore because they were told that the cash value of life insurance policy accumulates at 3 percent to 5 percent tax deferred.

Jack and Jill make the following conclusions:

- Traditional investment products will not help them achieve their goals.
- They don't understand the stock market. They have a very limited amount of money to invest.
- They are nowhere near the amount needed for a home down payment.

They decided that they will do further research on each of these areas.

## High Risk

Some people are impulsive and impatient, so they go all in to achieve their desired goals. They are not willing to create a progressive plan to achieve their goals over time. They are actually willing to risk everything on the potential of immediate results. Unfortunately, this can also lead to very rash decisions, which may be made without the proper consideration of methodology or consequence.

Emotionally charged decisions are often an impediment to success.

We all know people who constantly take chances based on raw emotion heavily laced with personal desire. This approach gave birth to the question, "What were you thinking?"

### *What Were They Thinking?*

- the persons who takes all of the equity out of his or her home and uses the entire amount to buy tickets in the mega lottery
- the person who has no income, assets, savings, or guarantee of work but still moves away from his or her family
- the person who skydives for the first time with no training and no focus on safety precautions
- the teenager who uses a gun to hold up the local liquor store to get money to buy drugs
- the man or woman who has unprotected sex with a stranger
- the employee who does not show up for work for three days without any communication with his or her employer
- the person who jumps off a cliff into a pond without first checking the depth of the water

You can add your personal examples to this endless list. Impulsive actions can often lead to unexpected and unwanted consequences.

To properly manage risk, a person must take the appropriate precautions to prevent as many unexpected or unwanted influences from derailing the success of the mission.

Taking risks may involve potential physical, mental, or emotional harm to you and others. Preventive planning is needed prior to any action, especially high-risk ventures.

History shows us that bold thinkers advance society by giving the world new tools to evolve. They think big and are willing to take enormous risks for substantial gains.

Look at each risk listed in the table below and identify the risk level you think applies.

*Risk Tolerance Quiz L (Low risk)  M (Moderate risk)      H (High risk)*

_____ Leaving your current job to start your own business

_____ Changing the color or style of your hair

_____ Climbing Mount Everest

_____ Purchasing a new home

_____ Going ice-skating for the first time

_____ Investing a small amount of money in the stock

_____ Lending money to a friend or family member

_____ Getting a divorce

_____ Having another child

_____ Buying an office building with a partner

_____ Changing your childhood religion for another faith

_____ Traveling as a tourist to a politically unstable foreign country

Never believe anything is *risk free*. Influences beyond your control are always present.

Everything you do comes with a potential element of risk. Spontaneous actions can be damning.

The counterpoint is also true: too much analysis usually leads to no action at all. If you do not take risks, you do not evolve. You never take advantage of the countless opportunities that cross your path.

Every action you take defines who you are. Let me say it again: every action you take defines who you are or who you want to be. This also includes what you fail to do.

Make sure the risks you are planning to take have been identified, well-defined, and well researched and that your decision to move forward warrants taking a chance.

## The F-Word

*Failure: the greatest teacher of all*

Failure is a daily occurrence for everyone. No one wins all the time. That would make compatible living with others impossible. You might have failed in your work, which led your life in a new direction. You might have failed in a marriage but you've found a new person who is more compatible with your likes and dislikes. You may have failed in your spiritual life, which forced you to explore developing a more meaningful relationship with God.

You cannot understand success if you have never failed. Each failure is an announcement of a new direction in your life. Each failure causes you to redefine who you are and who you want to be.

See each failure as a life lesson and a motivator to seek change. Every change is actually a positive step toward your personal evolution.

Do not excessively dwell on your losses. Change them into opportunities!

## Timeless Wisdom

*"A journey begins with a single step." (Confucius)*

Every great journey started with a thought manifested into an idea. You have thousands of thoughts every day, and no doubt many ideas spring forth from those thoughts. However, no thought or idea is really valuable unless it leads to action. Some dreamers simply dream while other dreamers who take action have built the world.

Impatience often pushes you to attempt to accomplish too much in too little time. Some very important aspects of life cannot be rushed. They need to be nurtured to grow.

To start a new journey, simply take one step and then another. Repeat this process continuously to embrace the marvels of a lifetime. Do not look back. Look only slightly ahead to prevent the panic of overestimating your progress. When you look too far ahead, you might miss the need of now. You may really scare yourself into believing that the ultimate goal is impossible to achieve. You might stop your journey just before reaching your desired destination.

Enjoy each step of the journey, knowing you are just a little closer to your final destination.

*Mistakes are the by-product of effort.*

A meaningful life is lived by trial and error. Every new experience requires trying new things. This can lead to mistakes. The secret is to learn from errors and then make a commitment not to make that mistake again.

Think opportunity and evolve.

Opportunities encourage growth. Growth is a small step in the journey of evolution. Do not miss opportunities because of fear and doubt.

If you do the same error repeatedly, it's not a mistake. It has become an intentional act.

*Nothing happens until you take strategic action.*

All great ideas crash and burn because of a lack of action. Ideas backed by effort have a reasonably good chance of succeeding.

Ready, set, *go!*

Opportunities keep kicking you in the head. Wake up!

# Never Confuse Effort with Results

You often hear people say things like, "I work so damn hard, but I can't seem to make any progress." Another common statement is, "I work as hard or even harder than my manager but get paid less. It's unfair." Often people confuse the significant difference between effort and results.

To illustrate this point, let's review the example below.

*Story: The Deadly Assumption*

Whenever you are frustrated because things are not working out for you, even though you are putting out a maximum amount of effort, go out to your garage and step over to the windowsill. Look down and you will observe a variety of insects that clutter the shelf below the window. See if you can spot the star of our example—the moth.

The moth probably entered the garage when the garage door was ajar or the side door was open. Finding nothing tasty to support its garage adventure, the moth seeks to find an open escape. It spies only the garage window, which appears to be a grand exit. The moth darts toward the light only to discover that rather than an express route to freedom, the moth's path is blocked by an unknown and invisible shield.

After the moth bounces off the glass, it determines that more effort needs to be applied. The moth continually repeats the attempt to get through the window, failing each time. *More effort, just more effort,* it thinks. With each new attempt, the moth tries with greater energy but makes absolutely no progress. The moth is now very exhausted, demoralized, and injured. Eventually the moth, as if trapped in a bottle, expires from hunger, energy loss, and injuries.

Another moth finds the window with the same plan of escape. Despite the array of dead insects cluttering the windowsill, the newly arrived insect starts its own dance of death.

Effort was not the problem. There were no results.

Had the moth only realized the futility of its efforts, it would have flown around the garage looking for viable options. Because the moth just increased its efforts to power through the window, never actually exploring other potential options, its fate was sealed.

How many times have you found yourself acting out your own scenario in a similar fashion? When you did not succeed with a certain methodology, you increased your intensity, performing the same actions with more effort. Maybe applying more effort isn't always the best way to solve a problem.

Now you know the lesson of effort versus result. You also understand the true definition of insanity, doing the same thing in the same way over and over and expecting a different result.

## Desired Result

Before embarking on any journey, it is imperative that you determine the specific result you are seeking. What is it that you are attempting to accomplish?

Before the journey, determine the following:

- what you want to achieve
- why you want to achieve it
- when you want to accomplish your goal
- who can help you get results
- how you want to achieve your desired goal (method)
- how you will measure your progress and end results

It seems like a lot of work needs to be done before you take your first step. The alternative is to just start and hope for the best.

Time and time again, you have taken action without the proper amount of preparation, which probably led to disappointment. Creating a strategy can be invigorating. It builds confidence, enthusiasm, and a sincere commitment to your goal.

## Clarifying Your Preferences

Have you outlined the specific person you want as your life companion? Probably not! Most people let their body chemistry take charge in selecting a partner. Mutual chemistry is important in every relationship, but much more is needed for the survival of a sustainable and mutually beneficial relationship.

The type of chart below can be used on any goal. For the sake of this example, let's assume you're a single female trying to determine what she would like in a life companion. Being very specific about what you want will alert your senses. It sends a message to the universal forces to provide you with your desired outcome.

Take the following quiz. Circle your preference in each category and then rank each item from 1 to 5 (1 being low priority, 3 about average priority, and 5 a high priority).

| Rank | Topic | Options – Circle one per element | | | | |
|---|---|---|---|---|---|---|
| ____ | Height | 5'6" | 5'10" | 6'0" | 6'3" | 6'5" |
| ____ | Weight | 150 lbs | 175 lbs | 190 lbs | 210 lbs | 240 lbs |
| ____ | Build | Athletic | Thin | Trim | Thick | Buff |
| ____ | Skin | Fair | Rosy | Tan | Dark | Black |
| ____ | Hair Color | Blond | Red | Light brown | Dark brown | Black |
| ____ | Facial Hair | Clean | Moustache | Beard | Goatee | Other |
| ____ | Unique | Tattoo | Piercings | Glasses | Jewels | Other |
| ____ | Eyes | Brown | Hazel | Blue | Green | Other |
| ____ | Age | 25-35 | 36-45 | 46-55 | 56-65 | 65+ |
| ____ | Religion | Christian | Islamic | Jewish | Hindu | Agnostic |
| ____ | Habits | Smoker | Nonsmoker | Drinker | Nondrinker | Other |
| ____ | Job | Local | Travels often | White collar | Blue collar | Risky |
| ____ | Previous Life | Divorced | Single | Widowed | Has kids | Zero kids |
| ____ | Goals | Money | Family | Travel | Sport | Retire |
| ____ | Interests | Theater | Outdoors | Travel | Sports | Arts |
| ____ | Education | High school | Jr. college | BA or BS | MA/MBA | PhD |

This chart is neither comprehensive nor standardized. It simply demonstrates your ability to determine your preferences. This approach enables you to subconsciously be aware of the compatibility and attraction you might have with people you encounter.

## Nonnegotiable Choice Eliminators

Whenever you make a decision, you need to be mindful of any potential choice eliminators. A choice eliminator is an element of such high importance that its absence will eliminate an option.

A young woman falls in love with an older man who has children from a previous marriage. The young woman wants to have children, but her older lover is firm that he wants no more kids. The outcome? *choice eliminator.*

You are of strong religious belief. Your religion is very important to you. You meet someone who thinks your religion is meaningless. Outcome: *choice eliminator.*

You had a previous relationship in which your partner had a compulsive personality, which was demonstrated through smoking, heavy drinking, occasional drug use, and infidelity. Your new partner has the very same issues. Outcome: *choice eliminator.*

If you knowingly ignore choice eliminators, you have chosen to ignore your own better judgment. You have set yourself up for disappointment or worse.

It takes both wisdom as well as courage to step away from a situation that gives you a warning signal like a choice eliminator.

Without a methodology for determining what you want and what you truly do not want, you will stumble from one situation to another.

How many daytime television programs have you seen in which one person in a committed relationship cheats on his or her partner? Invariably the harmed partner rejects the common-sense conclusion that the relationship is toxic and needs to end. He or she often takes back the cheater by rationalizing the negative behavior.

Can someone change his or her negative behavior into positive behavior? Yes, of course. The question is, do you want him or her to go through that change at your expense? Do you deserve the pain of such a process, hoping true change occurs? You deserve better!

Good results come from planning followed by execution. Do not ignore choice eliminators.

Good results come from a clear vision of the destination or goal. Once the goal is known, working backward, you can easily ascertain the appropriate journey and needed timeline. Catapulting into action without preparation is unwise. Results are often a long time in coming. That is why *resilience* is a key element in achieving successful results.

> *Develop success from failures. Discouragement and failure are two of the surest stepping-stones to success.*
> —Dale Carnegie

## Story: Practice Leads to Excellence

As a coach, it became clear to me that my athletes loved to compete but they really did not like to practice or train. To get the desired results, you must continually practice. You must fail periodically. You must learn from your failures. You must not give up your dream at the first sign of opposition or difficulty. You must make failure your friend and your teacher.

Hard work is a critical element of any success, but it is not a guarantee of success. Hard work is admirable but expected as a fundamental and common element for anyone to succeed. Many people work hard doing things that don't work, still hoping to reach their desired goals.

So it is a combination of many things that brings about successful results, not the least of which is experience.

> *Our greatest weakness lies in giving up. The most certain way to succeed is always to try just one more time.*
> —Thomas Edison

## Lesson Learned

You can't get results without hard work, but hard work alone does not automatically guarantee results without practice, vision, and adaptability.

# The F-Word

*Focus: the narrowness of passionate determination*

You are part of a generation of people who have been brought up on the concept that multitasking is both necessary and a very good trait. Certainly at times, the ability to handle more than one thing at once is sorely needed. Parents working with their children are great examples of this very need.

Oftentimes, attempting numerous things at one time creates errors that could have been avoided with more focus. Businesses spend huge amounts of money every year to correct the errors of employees caused by lapses in judgment, overwhelming workloads, unnecessary duplications, and sloppy work performance. The overall cost of correcting these issues is astronomical. These expenses are passed on to the customers in the form of higher prices for products and services.

The very important things you hope to accomplish in life, those things that you are passionate about, need your extreme attention.

In your scattered attempt to be good at everything, you may become average at everything. Selecting only a few things in your life toward which you devote all of your passion is the way to find great personal rewards.

Being focused is very important, but that focus must also be linked with an awareness of its impact on those around you. Your focus can never shut a child away from your time or a spouse from your love.

Focus today will bring great rewards somewhere in the future.

# Timeless Wisdom

*Never succumb to negative thinkers.*

Negative people always lean toward the impossible. Sadly, they discourage progress. They feel the need to convert all optimistic people into doubters and skeptics.

Negative thinking is the darkest side of life. Reject and resist those who want to restrict your journey and limit your opportunity to soar.

Negative thinkers rarely smile.

*Maturity is not a matter of age, it is a combination of experience and reflection.*

There is no substitute for experience, but experience that is devoid of reflection does not become wisdom. Wisdom is the marriage of experience and reflection.

*Analysis after an action is where true learning takes place.*

You need to carve out an appropriate amount of time after any experience to review what went well, what went wrong, what you would do again, and what you would change. This regular fine-tuning methodology constantly moves you to a better level of performance.

If you become a little lost or things are not working well for you, seek out an experienced person to mentor you and give you ideas. That mentor might give you that little piece of advice that turns your progress around.

Do not overlook any learning opportunity.

# Having a Sense of Humor

## Rules of Humor

- Never lose the merriment of life.
- See the lightness all around you.
- Laugh often and hard.
- Never laugh at someone.
- Mischief eases tension.
- Practical jokes are not practical.
- Laugh at yourself.
- Make others smile and laugh often.
- Hang out with children more often.
- Eat a snow cone once in a while.
- Do not take yourself or others too seriously.
- Make everything an opportunity for fun.

---

*A Canadian psychologist is selling a video that teaches you how to test your dog's IQ. Here's how it works: If you spend $12.99 for the video, your dog is smarter than you.*

—Jay Leno

---

*We need a twelve-step group for compulsive talkers. They could call it On Anon Anon.*

—Paula Poundstone

## The F-Word

*Funny: the art of identifying the lightness of life*

Comedians make us laugh by finding the humor, light side, or irony of the behavior you see every day but may have missed because you were absorbed with other matters.

Ellen DeGeneres is an expert observer who can capture the humor in the simplest act. Check out her standup routine on tripping while walking. She describes and demonstrates the wacky things people do to cover their mistake. You will be able to relate to every one of her observations. You will laugh at her delivery and the depth of her introspection. I love her humor because I have done many of the cover-ups she demonstrates, so I can relate to her material, which by the way, is devoid of vulgarity. Well done, Ellen!

*My grandmother started walking five miles a day when she was sixty. She's ninety-seven now, and we don't know where the hell she is.*

—Ellen DeGeneres

Humor can lighten tense moments. Humor actually unites diverse individuals into a relaxed commonality, temporarily putting their worries on hold.

Children laugh hundreds of times a day. They take great joy in their own produced humor and the humor they see in others. There is really no greater sound in the world than the sound of a child's laughter.

Unfortunately, by the time these happy children become adults, they laugh infrequently.

Have we lost our sense of humor, or is it simply hidden under layers of stress and reality?

Break this current trend by smiling. Make life a joyful experience. Laugh often! Laugh loudly!

> *Procrastination isn't a problem, it's the solution. So procrastinate now, don't put it off.*
>
> —Ellen DeGeneres

You can win a person over with a sincere smile and a little laughter. Everyone wants to be around someone who is fun and does not take him- or herself too seriously.

So, a guy walks into a bar … This introduction gets my wife laughing even before I get to the joke. She already anticipates that a good laugh is on the way.

## Timeless Wisdom

*Be blessed by a child's laughter.*

Find the humor in all things. Laughter lightens the soul and decompresses the most stressful situation.

Laugh often and with gusto.

*Listen with an open mind.*

You will not act on every idea that is presented to you, but you owe it to your fellow collaborators to let each idea be voiced and truly considered. Rejecting an idea without examination will stifle the desire of others to volunteer their thoughts.

Calm your mind. Things will be fine.

*Enjoy your life with laughter and anticipation.*

Have you seen the joy in the face of a child when they eat some cotton candy or are told they are going to a park? They giggle and dash to the car. They enjoy simple things and block out the stress of adult mind babble. Let the child in you come out often!

> *Just go up to somebody on the street and say, "You're it!" and just run away.*
>
> —Ellen DeGeneres

# Yesterday, Today, Tomorrow

**D**o you use your time effectively? Do you have a process of time use, priority setting, results measurement, and behavioral modification that will improve your life, your enjoyment, your income and your professional career?

Let's take a moment to view two sales representatives who sell the exact same products, work in similar markets, and have comparable skills. What they do not have in common is their processes, level of success, or incomes.

## Yesterday

Tom is pleasant with his clients. He is honest and works hard. He arrives at work and immediately jumps on the phone to set appointments. He visits about three clients per day. He always wraps up the day at 5:30 p.m., when he arrives home to be with his family.

Tom's sales are average, as is his income. He often meets with his sales manager about his marginal sales results. He is not viewed as part of the long-range plan of his company, and he has never been considered for a leadership position.

Frank, on the other hand, comes into the office every day at 8:00 a.m. The first thing he does is pull out a blank yellow pad of paper, on which he writes several of the things he did yesterday that worked. He reflects on his successes and enjoys measuring how those sales will improve his position within the sales team and how much income he generated from his efforts.

Next, he writes down what did not work well yesterday. After he is brutally honest with himself, he determines what he might have done incorrectly. What needs to be changed?

Then he writes down what he wants to continue to do and the things that need to be altered.

On a simple three-by-five-inch index card, Frank writes down any question or objection he received yesterday that he felt he did not handle effectively. On the back of the card, he then writes what he would like to say the next time he is asked that same question (This can also be done electronically) He words his response to make it an open-ended question. Frank knows whoever is asking the question is in charge of the interview.

Finally, Frank writes out his three most important priorities for the day. He will intentionally share these three priorities with his team upon their arrival. The entire team knows Frank's priorities.

At 9:00 a.m., Frank gets on the phone to set appointments. Because he analyzed his recent experience, he knows he will be more effective today.

Frank's three goals have given him both a purpose for the day and direction on the use of his time.

Tom merely jumps into daily tasks right where he left off yesterday.

## Today

Tom starts at the top of the alphabet and begins to call. When he has confirmed three appointments, he stops calling and leaves the office to make sales calls and presentations. Unfortunately, all three of the willing clients who agreed to see Tom are low volume buyers.

At 5:30 p.m., Tom arrives home to his family. When his family asks about his day, he shares that he made sales with each of the three appointments he scheduled for today for a sales volume of approximately $3,000.

Frank has decided he will make four sales today with a collected sales volume of $10,000. Frank knows that he will not be able to achieve his goal if he spends the bulk of his day with low volume purchasing clients. He immediately identifies three of his top accounts to visit. He adds in a new, smaller account that is just starting in the business but who has great future sales potential.

After Frank's last appointment, he returns to the office to process all of the sales paperwork so he can get paid as quickly as possible. He saw all four clients. Two of the high volume customers purchased a little over $12,000 of merchandise collectively. One of his very high volume customers purchased nothing. The smaller, newer client made a purchase of $1,000, which was actually more than Frank expected. The total sales for Frank was $13,000, which exceeded his $10,000 goal by an amount equal to Tom's total sales volume for the day ($3,000).

## Tomorrow

Tom will come into the office and repeat what he did the day before.

Frank will measure his results against his five-year plan. He will report his very successful day to his manager and share how the day improved the total results of the team.

He will glance at the picture he has on his desk of Pebble Beach Lodge, which will be his reward if he is the top salesperson in his area. He knows that making this trip will allow him to meet and visit with the president of the company, who has already sent feelers out to him about possibly moving into a leadership role.

Both Tom and Frank will work hard today. Both spend similar time on the job. Both leave their homes each morning with the intention of selling a high volume of product.

What makes the difference?

**Yesterday**        Goal - Analysis and Performance

Tom spent no time spent reviewing what worked, making adjustments, or creating solutions.

Frank reviewed his actual performance, made adjustments, created solutions, and increased his efficiency.

**Today**        Goal - Execution of the plan to achieve the goal

Tom did not have a plan or a goal that would define a successful day.

Frank had specific goals, planned the day to fit the goals, and measured his results at the end of the day.

**Tomorrow**              Goal - Vision of the future

Tom does not have a five-year plan or even a career goal. He is adrift and floats from one possible sale to another. His lack of purpose and direction makes him an unlikely long-term employee of his present company.

Frank has specific immediate and long-term plans. He measures his performance daily against his goals. He knows at all times where he is against the competition. He also knows his standing among the sales team.

To be successful and to sustain your success, you need to devote time daily to all three of these areas: yesterday, today, and tomorrow.

It is suggested you spend at least 10 percent of your day on yesterday (analysis); 80 percent of your day on today (plan execution); and 10 percent of your day on tomorrow (reviewing your results against your vision and goals).

This will take a realignment of your daily schedule. This will mean a change in the priorities of each day. If your actions do not support your goals, you are doomed to failure and disappointment.

How you set your goals, analyze your performance, and measure your results against your vision will determine your ability to achieve your dreams.

# The F-Word

*Future: the many consequences of yesterday and the unpredictable surprises of tomorrow*

The future is bright for all who have spent the time reading this material, but only if they apply what they have learned. That is the secret of the future, to plan where you go and what you want to do, avoid distractions, and then take strategic action to complete your plan.

The future for all of us will be an endless series of hills and valleys. It is just the nature of life on this planet. Those who prepare and then adapt to life's variables are in a better position to evolve over those who hope for the best and do nothing to make the best happen.

If you learn from your experiences, suppress your fears, and call forth optimistic outcomes, you will have the greatest success.

The future is the desired destination of dreamers, innovators, builders, and the emotionally intelligent. Great things are within your grasp if you remove the myths you have created for yourself.

Turn your knowledge into wisdom through experience and reflection.

*You determine your future!*

This is your life, so live it your way! Determine your own boundaries, plan your personal road map, enjoy each step of the journey, and then hold on for the most exciting and thrilling adventure you can imagine.

## Timeless Wisdom

*Happiness is not a continuous state of being; it is a periodic experience buffered by stages of waiting.*

Life goes in cycles of pain, comfort, and happiness, only to be repeated over and over again.

Survey one hundred people and you will find that at least one person is entering into a major life crisis, such as an illness, the loss of a job, or a broken marriage. At least one other person is just coming out of a life crisis. The remaining 98 percent are somewhere in between. You see, this is how we learn and grow. We need to know pain to appreciate love. We need to know cold to understand warmth.

We live in a world of duality, designed to help us understand both sides of the living experience.

Nothing lasts forever.

*There is nothing more valuable than your health.*

It is correctly said that the body is the temple of the spirit. A healthy body enables its owner to experience the fullness of life. The person who is physically limited is restricted from expressing all the desires of the soul. People limited by undesired difficulties simply find new outlets to express their souls' intentions.

Keeping yourself in good health should be a critical priority for everyone. Good health dramatically improves energy, enthusiasm, desire, ability, and emotional balance.

Rest the mind and exercise the body as a selfish act for you and you alone.

*Change is inevitable so meet it head on.*

Change is constant. It will happen with or without you. Make change your friend. Face change with excitement, knowing that new opportunities loom in your future.

Bring on the change!

# Conclusion and Action

The purpose of this book is to give you knowledge, wisdom, and tools to handle your everyday experiences. It is a daunting task to remain balanced and centered in such an overly complicated world. You will not be able to control all of the elements that create your existence, but you can choose your reaction to them. You control the creation of your *brand*. You control the *choices* you make on every issue. You control whether you *adapt* and *evolve*.

Slow down and heighten your *awareness*. Spend time *observing*! You will be amazed at how much reality, joy, and life you have been missing.

Better your life by cherishing each experience to support better choices in the future.

Take a moment to write down just three important things you want to implement. Remember, knowledge without meaningful action is simply wasted. Share your three goals or objectives with someone you trust and someone who will be honest with you. Ask them to visit with you to periodically measure your progress and refocus your attention, if necessary, to successfully achieve your goals.

Life is a contact sport to be experienced, not merely observed. Take a calculated risk to grow, prosper, adapt, and evolve.

Know that the only way you can coast through life is always downhill.

Focused action, on the other hand, will drive you up the next mountain to enjoy all of the wonderful things that are on the horizon.

This is your life! Live it your way!

Leave no love unspent. Enjoy each sunset and eagerly anticipate the coming dawn. Great things are just ahead!

# ABOUT THE AUTHOR

Lloyd "Skip" Amstrup earned a bachelor's degree in political science from San Jose State University. He taught high school students for eight years and worked in the insurance industry for thirty-two years, retiring as a field executive for State Farm. He was born in San Francisco and grew up in Columbus, Ohio. He and Trica, his wife, have two children and five grandchildren.

## Open Book Editions
## A Berrett-Koehler Partner

Open Book Editions is a joint venture between Berrett-Koehler Publishers and Author Solutions, the market leader in self-publishing. There are many more aspiring authors who share Berrett-Koehler's mission than we can sustainably publish. To serve these authors, Open Book Editions offers a comprehensive self-publishing opportunity.

### A Shared Mission

Open Book Editions welcomes authors who share the Berrett-Koehler mission— Creating a World That Works for All. We believe that to truly create a better world, action is needed at all levels—individual, organizational, and societal. At the individual level, our publications help people align their lives with their values and with their aspirations for a better world. At the organizational level, we promote progressive leadership and management practices, socially responsible approaches to business, and humane and effective organizations. At the societal level, we publish content that advances social and economic justice, shared prosperity, sustainability, and new solutions to national and global issues.

Open Book Editions represents a new way to further the BK mission and expand our community. We look forward to helping more authors challenge conventional thinking, introduce new ideas, and foster positive change.

For more information, see the Open Book Editions website:
http://www.iuniverse.com/Packages/OpenBookEditions.aspx

Join the BK Community! See exclusive author videos, join discussion groups, find out about upcoming events, read author blogs, and much more! http://bkcommunity.com/